THE SKILLS
OF MANAGEMENT

THE SKILLS
OF MANAGEMENT

A. N. Welsh

**A DIVISION OF
AMERICAN MANAGEMENT ASSOCIATIONS**

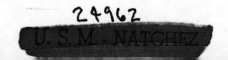

Library of Congress Cataloging in Publication Data

Welsh, A.N.
  The skills of management.

  Includes Index.
  1. Management.   I. Title.
HD31.W462   1981   658   80-69694
ISBN 0-8144-5670-7

First published by Gower Press, England. © 1979 A. N. Welsh

Published in the United States in 1981 by AMACOM,
a division of American Management Associations, New York.
All rights reserved. Printed in the United States of America.

First Printing

Acknowledgments

In the interests of being concise, I have made very few references and acknowledgments in this book, and I hope I may be forgiven any omissions. Nevertheless, I must thank Mrs. Pat Moss for her many hours of work on the drafts, and Mr. David Moss, her husband, of the Plessey Company, who provided much of the inspiration for Chapter 17. I owe a substantial debt to my former employers, W. D. Scott & Company, for their forbearance and for all my experience with them. I must thank Mr. Michael Owen and the Air Transport and Travel Industry Training Board for permission to draw from management training material developed while I was with W. D. Scott, and I owe a special debt for encouragement to Philip Stott, Sydney Paulden, Peter Zentner, and to my long-suffering wife, Jennifer.

A. N. WELSH

Contents

		Introduction and Study Plan	1
Part I		**Managing Yourself**	
	1	Personal Organization / Part One	7
	2	Personal Organization / Part Two	11
	3	Management and Leadership Styles	20
	4	Personal Impact	27
	5	Objectives	32
Part II		**Managing Others**	
	6	Planning and Scheduling	41
	7	The Decision-Making Process	56
	8	Meetings and Reports	66
	9	Motivation	77
	10	Persuasion and Selling	87
Part III		**Additional Techniques**	
	11	Recruitment: Selection and Induction	103
	12	Appraisal and Counseling	115
	13	Teaching and Learning	125
	14	The Assessment and Improvement of Work	130
	15	Causes of Difference in Output	144
	16	Manpower Planning and Control	158
	17	The Manager and the Trade Unions	171
		Summary and Work Plan	181
		Index	185

When all else fails, read the directions.

OLD CHINESE PROVERB

Introduction and Study Plan

THIS BOOK is intended for practicing managers and for those who have to understand and assess the management of others. In this book, *management* means the management of people, how to make them do what you want, how to reconcile the objectives of the enterprise with their own needs and aspirations, and how to use their own time to the best advantage.

The method of the book is to describe practical tips and methods, to illustrate them and the learning process, and then to reinforce them by exercises under each subject heading and by suggestions for action to be taken. Management is at least partly learned on the job, and factors such as example, compulsion, and persuasion have to be seen in practice. The book aims at simulating this practice, and is therefore specific rather than general in most of its areas.

Nevertheless, most good managers know that one of the main secrets of success lies in preparation, and this book may be viewed as a component of the manager's preparation. The management writer F. W. Taylor equated management with control, and he said that control could exist only in the presence of three prerequisites: first, that

STUDY PLAN

Chapter	Subject	Time to read (hrs)	Time for exercises (hrs)	Date planned	Date actual	Review/ reread

you know what staff people should be doing; second, that they know how they should be doing it; and third, that they know how long it should take. This book will be concerned with the will to manage and the will to be managed but it will treat all Taylor's prerequisites in some depth.

Observers of the management scene will be uncomfortably aware that all too many executives are not able to give a clear answer as to what they should be doing, how and why they should be doing it, and according to what sort of timetable. Perhaps one of the biggest problems that results from this is that individual managers begin to feel that their scope is limited, and as a result they lose confidence. If this book can make it possible for some of that confidence to return by showing managers just how they can achieve difficult or seemingly impossible tasks, then its purposes will have been achieved.

The book is in three parts. The first part is the organization of the manager as a person, how he makes the best use of himself and of his time, how he improves his decision making, and how he relates to other people. The second part relates to the actual mechanics of management: how the manager directs his function to achieve results; how he organizes tasks, discussions, meetings, and reports; and how he makes or receives communications above and below. The third part is a mixture of techniques that the manager may find helpful in his executive capacity. These include financial and manpower controls and statistics, organization and method techniques, selling, teaching, and assessment of output.

There are 17 chapters in this book. It should take you approximately half an hour to read each one and an additional half-hour to complete each set of exercises. In a particularly complex area, the exercises might take one to two hours. Why not work out a reading plan for yourself based on spending one evening or morning (or whenever you can regularly make the time free) per week for the next seventeen weeks? Complete one section at a time. Do not leave a chapter half-finished, but do not burden yourself by trying to do more than one at a time. You can use the chart on the opposite page to keep track of your progress.

This book is a distillation of a great deal of experience and of management development work. If you work through it as suggested, you will increase your managerial self-awareness—and at a low cost.

One point I should like to add. Increasing numbers of women are obtaining supervisory and managerial positions, and this book is for them also. I may have appeared to address my remarks to men, but this is because of the nature of our English language, where, for better or worse, and as in other circumstances, the masculine embraces the feminine.

PART

I

MANAGING YOURSELF

I had forgotten to do. I had the choice then of lying awake the rest of the night and remembering whatever it was, or going to sleep again and forgetting the matter, although I had not really forgotten it. At least I did not decide to hold a meeting about the situation!

CREATING A LIST

I listed all the jobs that I had to do, all the work in my "in" box, and all the functions that I had to supervise. I kept a diary, and a current file (which, in my case, was a concertina file with slots for the days 1–31 and for the remaining months of the year). To the current file I would add any correspondence, assessments, buying orders, and the like which I wanted to review at a future date; these items were brought into the list as they came up. Having made the first rough list, I then sorted it into its order of importance and urgency. At the end of each day, I used to go through the list and cross off what I had done and also any items which were no longer relevant. I would add to the list any new jobs or problems that had arisen, and then I would note which jobs I planned to do the following day.

So, in the morning, there was my list telling me what I had to do that day. Obviously, unexpected matters arose (in an operational situation one can almost budget for the unexpected), but by and large I worked through the list each day.

COMMUNICATIONS

One of the standing items on the list, apart from going through the diary and current file, was to see all my subordinates. I kept at hand a list of all subordinates, and made a point of seeing each one—even if only to say hello—every day. It could be, of course, that you are often away, or that you have too many staff people to see. Perhaps in the first case you should consider whether you are away too much to do your job properly; in the second case, you may have too many people directly under you and you should delegate some of the communications process to subordinates. Communications is the name of this game: people require regular contact, in particular from their boss. They will often tell you things or, in talking with them, you

Read not to contradict or confute; nor to believe and take for granted; nor to find talk and discourse; but to weigh and consider.   FRANCIS BACON

1   Personal Organization
Part One

THE NEED FOR PERSONAL ORGANIZATION

When I had my first managerial job, I found it naturally very exciting and very demanding. I would come in on time, or even early. (To digress, a good manager should sometimes come in early and perhaps stay late. All sorts of things happen outside normal working hours. For example, people who get their work wrong or do not complete it during the day will stay behind or come back later to finish it off, while others will use company facilities for private purposes.) However, I would come in on time or early and work like mad throughout the day, but by the end I had never completed all that had to be done, and my head was full of everything that was happening. In particular, I was concerned by matters affecting the well-being of others, and also by attacks on my department's activities or on my own standards of performance.

When I arrived home, my head was buzzing and I would wake up in the middle of the night thinking of new ideas or remembering things may be able to sense a problem that they would be reluctant to bring to your office.

As an aside, what does your office look like to a subordinate? Can he obtain access to you easily, or are you involved most of the time in meetings, deep discussions, or telephone calls? Communications can only exist on a face-to-face basis, and they are of prime importance at every level. Many managers who have considerable responsibilities in large organizations do not know the names or faces of their top management and directors. An even greater proportion never see, or are never seen by, their top management in any operational situation. No amount of personnel work can make people think you care about them if they never see you!

PERSONAL PLANNING

The first list of work is much more difficult to produce than the subsequent amendments, and, to help you produce it there is a list of questions at the end of the chapter. These are general and analytical questions to be used in any review of your responsibilities, but they would assist in preparing the first list. When, you may ask, would you ever have time to do this? Is it possible with everyone rampaging around and the phone ringing?

However, do you intend to spend the rest of your life in a managerial pigsty, and are you seriously going to say you are too busy to do your job? Half an hour of planning or forethought can save hours or even days of misdirected effort. The crisis anticipated is no panic, and you should find in the normal situation that if you pursue this kind of personal planning for a few months, you will get "ahead of the game," and you can then start looking for additional responsibilities.

Decide now on a specific half-hour in the coming week to go through the list. Ask someone else to take the calls and say you do not want to be disturbed (unless the chairman is calling, of course). Some of the questions will be the subject of later chapters in the book or will require further investigation, but whenever the answer you reach is other than satisfactory, ask yourself, "What am I going to do about it?"

One common difficulty is that old sinking feeling that although problems could be put right if one only had the time, one *never* has the time—and never will have it, either. The next chapter offers some suggestions on this point.

Checklist for Reviewing Your Function

1. What are the objectives of my department or function?
2. Do I feel that these can be achieved—that I have a plan for this?
3. In what ways can my department or area be improved?
4. Is the work in my area altering in nature, quantity, or quality?
5. Can the work be done in a better way?
6. Have I the right equipment and facilities?
7. Have I the right number of people on staff?
8. Am I happy that all my subordinates are correctly placed?
9. Is my staff doing what I want it to do?
10. Do any of the people on my staff need further training or experience? Have I a training plan?
11. What are the staffing trends?
12. Are the people on my staff happy? Do I spend enough time with them?
13. Have I trained a deputy?
14. Am I satisfied personally? Have I defined my personal objectives?
15. Is my authority defined and adequate?
16. Is my relationship with my senior management satisfactory?
17. Where is my next promotion coming from?
18. Am I doing too much routine or administrative clerical work?
19. Have I enough time for thinking?

The slothful man saith, there is a lion without, I shall be slain in the street.   PROVERBS 26:13

2 Personal Organization
Part Two

THE CONSTRAINT OF TIME

The best manager is the one who manages best. Managing is not easy, and it is conducted within a large number of constraints. What is your biggest constraint? Is it capital, working finance, material resources, machinery, property, or people? People can be a big limiting factor, but you can always train them. Are you limited by the presence of other aspects? Many factors can constrain you, but the biggest restriction of all is your own time: you never have enough of it. There are only 24 hours in a day, 7 days in a week, 52 weeks in the year, and so many years in your career. You cannot produce more time; it keeps slipping away. Yesterday can never come back.

We would say, therefore, that we do not have as much time as we need, but would this be equally true for everybody, or would it apply in particular to you? Time can be replaced. Certain tasks can be performed by machinery and certain office work can be done by computers. Some tasks can be delegated to other people, although this is really a transfer of time. However, the manager cannot delegate his management work to a machine and seldom can he share it with any-one else. There is no substitute for time as far as he is concerned. Everything he does takes time. All business, all activity, all work uses time and takes place in time.

However, we do not manage our time naturally; as a whole, we take it for granted. Now we could talk for a long time about this prob-lem, and we could say that the unhurried, unheroic manager with a clear desk and a reliable organized office is the efficient or effective manager, but what do you do about it?

Step 1. Accept that, other things being equal, the best and happiest manager is the one who makes the best use of his time. If you do not accept this, then this chapter was not written for you, but if you feel that you can make better use of time, and that if you do so you will be a better manager, then please read on.

Step 2. This includes finding out what you are doing now. A simple method of doing this is to list various activities that you perform, and record for a week or a fortnight how long you are spending on them. This can be done by using a simple daily diary sheet. The diary sheets are broken down into what is called a work distribution chart at the end of the period. The work distribution chart will show quite clearly what you are doing and what proportion of your time you are spend-ing on your various activities. A specimen manager's activity list, with the activities given for example only, is as follows:

1. Visiting customers.
2. Visiting suppliers.
3. Answering queries from staff over technical matters.
4. Handling customer complaints.
5. Planning and control work.
6. Training.
7. Supervision.
8. Reading mail.
9. Chasing overdue accounts.
10. Checking stocks and reordering.
11. Management meetings.
12. Recruiting.
13. Staff problems.
14. Personal.

Date:

Time	Activity	Inter-ruptions	Phone calls	1. Inessen-tial	2. Some-body else could do	3. Wast-ing others time	Notes
8:30 8:45 9:00 9:15 9:30 9:45 10:00 ,, ,, ,, ,, 5:30 5:45 6:00 Evening	Enter number against time whenever activity changes.	Enter a '1' for each, e.g. 1, 11	As for interruptions, note incidence and quantity. Analyze if too many.	Record impressions, if any, at the time.	Record impressions, if any, at the time.	Record impressions, if any, at the time.	Note anything unusual or "special."

Figure 2-1. Specimen manager's diary sheet.

Simple forms for the diary sheet and work distribution chart are shown in Figures 2-1 and 2-2.

The work of a manager is variable, particularly with regard to the subject involved. A work distribution chart exercise will not give a 100 percent accurate picture of what the manager does or should do, but it will give a representative view of the proportions of his time spent on various activities—for example, queries. (Accounts queries may relate to different transactions, but there will still be accounts queries.) Once the work distribution chart has been completed, one can then move on to the next step.

Step 3. The third step is the analysis of the work distribution chart. A number of questions need to be asked at this stage (see next page).

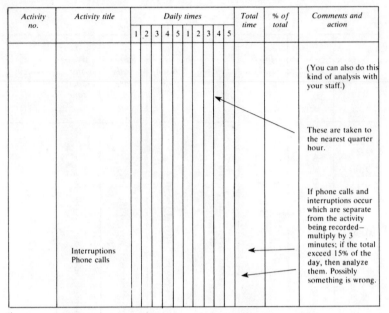

Figure 2-2. Manager's work distribution chart.

WASTED TIME

1. What would happen if I did not do this kind of activity?
2. Am I spending too much time on it?
3. Am I doing it ineffectively? For example, am I getting it properly set up and spending enough time on it? (Short periods of supervision are of limited value with persons engaged in complex work.)
4. Because of lack of time, am I failing to do any task that would contribute to the business?

A manager should be able to spend time with his staff—encouraging, training, supervising, and just getting to know them and keeping in touch. The time required for this varies with the staff and the complexity of the work, but a rough quick figure is an average of 40 minutes per person per day. This includes normal management duties, reports, and "personnel" work. It does not include checking as distinct from normal supervision and training.

Checking

Checking should be considered carefully. Twenty or thirty years ago, commercial convention looked for a high degree of literal accuracy, and salary costs were lower in proportion to other expenses than they are now. There is satisfaction in getting everything right and producing little masterpieces, but we should first consider what the customer really wants and needs. Checking is expensive and frustrating; it is no longer a motivating factor (if it ever was) for the staff to have all its work checked.

Your work distribution chart will show how much of your time is spent checking, but you should consider whether the cost of checking is justified by the errors discovered and how much these matter. If the errors do matter, you may have to continue the check, but you can consider whether random checks or occasional, unexpected checks will serve as well where general quality standards and methods are the main concern.

List of Jobs

In the end, you will finish with a list of the jobs which you want and have to do, and a subsidiary list of jobs which you feel you should not be doing but perhaps still have to do, for one reason or another. (We are, of course, well aware that you cannot get rid of all inessential tasks, but you can reduce them.) You will rank the list of jobs in order of importance to the business, and estimate what general proportion of your time and energy should be spent on each.

Once you have considered where time is being wasted on unnecessary work and where time could be saved by better personal organization and work methods, you should move to the next heading in your analysis of the work distribution chart.

DELEGATION

Ask yourself which of your activities could be done by somebody else—adequately, as well as you can, or even better than you can do it. The manager is paid to do his work, but if there are others at lower salaries who can do part of it and have the time to do it, then is it better for the manager or for the junior staff to be fully occupied?

Another factor which arises from this analysis is that the more senior people become, the larger becomes the proportion of their time spent on moving about and traveling, and you should take this into consideration.

There will be certain customers who are very important and who are accustomed to dealing with you personally. You may be able to introduce them to someone else who can deal with the routine parts of the account, but of course you must remember to watch what is happening to the account from time to time subsequent to this arrangement. This would apply also to important jobs and to important senior managers.

A few years back, the CEOs of several major companies in the United States were in very humble positions; in fact, consider where you yourself were five years ago, and now you are performing much more important work. Quite possibly within your area, you have got managers or senior managers of the future, and you should keep a look out for them and give them a chance as soon as you can. Not only will this be good for them, but it will also free you. Think about how to develop the business and to perform your other managerial tasks.

One thing which is very irksome to staff is to see people senior to them performing activities at greater salaries which they could do perfectly well themselves. In one major American company, the staff is asked the question, "What does your supervisor do that you could do yourself?" Could you ask this question of your staff, and would they know how to answer it? It is worth considering that they may have views on this subject themselves.

SUBORDINATES' TIME

A manager becomes a manager by promotion or appointment. He learns to be a manager by observing other managers, who themselves have learned by observation and what is called the "hard way." There are certain training courses, but they are normally very short, and as a result most managers devise their style and system of management from their own experience. Often this is very good, but once personal inclinations creep in, funny things start to happen.

You should ask yourself the following question: "Is there anything I do which wastes subordinates' time without contributing to their effectiveness?" You can begin to answer this question from your analysis of the work distribution chart, and you may even be able to ask it of the subordinates themselves.

Waiting Around

The kind of event we have in mind is where your staff has to hang around waiting for answers from you about items that need to be checked or approved or for action to be taken. Consider whether in your area you ever have two or more people involved in work that should be done by one person only. Normally speaking, it is more satisfying and efficient for a job that can be done by one person to be done by one person and not be split between two or three. Although it is true that the staff can learn from observing you, sometimes you may be playing to an audience unnecessarily (and distracting the others).

Remember back to when you were a worker or a member of the staff. Did your manager or foreman ever waste any of your time while you waited around for him to be available, when he was late, when he had to check your work, or when he was supposed to attend to something but was (or allowed himself to be) interrupted by a variety of other matters? Did this frustrate you as well as waste your time? Staff people are paid less than managers, but, with overheads, the difference is not as great as it once was. Are you working too hard? Are you paying the proverbial dog, and then doing the barking yourself?

Crises

One thing that wastes time, particularly of subordinates, is a crisis. In many organizations, crises occur regularly, and there are so many unforeseen events that one could almost describe crises as routine. However, a recurrent crisis is a symptom of slovenliness and laziness. Certain crises, such as making up the returns, the budget figures, sales figures, payroll, and peak season are all known in advance. If the manager uses some of the techniques suggested in Chapter 6, he may well be able to provide for these, in which case they will become routine occurrences and not crises.

Panicky action is expensive. People rushing off to make special deliveries, special visits to the post office, special trips to acquire stationery and other necessary supplies, people dropping things while picking up others—all these lead to an ineffective use of time and to mistakes.

IMPROVEMENTS

The question here is, how can you use your time more effectively? The first thing to consider is, what is your attention span? Are you a person who works best by sitting down quietly and for extended periods looking at a particular problem, or do you keep things running around in your mind? What are your best methods of working, and with whom and when?

Discretionary Time

You need to have a certain amount of discretionary time, that is, free time at your disposal, time available for important matters—perhaps the things you are paid for—and this must be kept in usable chunks. Not many managers feel they have much discretionary time, even after cutting out any wasted time, but they can generally set aside an hour or so each week. The question arises as to how much discretionary time is desirable. This is rather like maintenance on a car: you do not buy a car in order to service it, but if you do not carry out a certain amount of maintenance on the car, it will not perform satisfactorily.

Your Function

The same applies to your function. From time to time, you need to see the staff, to review the total operation of your area, and to go through the checklist in Chapter 1. On a daily basis you may want to keep a list of the tasks that you have to do and of the problems with deadlines and priorities, and perhaps revise these either the last thing at night or the first thing in the morning. Also you may well want to use a file or diary system so that you are automatically reminded of things that need doing in the future. How long this should take is like the service on the car, except that it is you rather than the garage that must make the diagnosis and the decisions.

Suggestions

Simple suggestions for using your time more effectively are to concentrate on one thing at a time; deal with first things first, and one at a time. Allow enough time for what you are doing—nothing ever goes completely right, and one thing you can always expect is the unexpected. Do not hurry, do not try to do several things at once, and do not assume that everything that was important yesterday will be important today. Ask yourself the question, "If we had not already started on this activity, would we start it now?" It is just as difficult and just as risky to do something small as it is to do something big, so allocate your time to the most important parts of the business.

When you have analyzed your work distribution chart and have compared the proportions of time spent on the various activities with their importance in terms of obtaining income, business, and profit or other advantage for the company, you will most certainly find that you are spending a lot of your time on small irritating matters. Consider whether some of these can be allowed to slide without damage to the business, and whether the situation would be improved by concentrating on the managerial areas of the business.

SUMMARY

To sum up, this chapter has offered certain suggestions for work on your own position. It has been suggested that the better manager is the better organized manager, who makes the best use of his time and best use of the time of his staff. However, just as there is no such thing as a born manager, so the effectiveness of a good manager cannot really be taught. Effectiveness has to be learned and the suggestions in this chapter are only some pointers about how to look at one's work, how to develop a style and personal approach, and how to make the best use of your time.

*Definition of a manager: one who pats you on the back
in front of your face, and then hits you below the belt
when your back is turned.*

3 Management and Leadership Styles

LOOKING BACK

My industrial career started in the early 1950s. As I remember life then—and it is not so long ago—a discussion on management styles would have been unusual. Work was underway on the behavioral aspects of business organization (especially by Douglas McGregor, Abraham Maslow, and Frederick Herzberg), but from a day-to-day point of view, management *per se* seemed a more obvious thing than it does now.

Business has grown more complex since then, but I started out with some of Great Britain's larger organizations. At that time, a manager—whether he was an office manager, a foreman, a plant manager, or a division manager—was a more recognizable entity. At different levels, managers had little ways of dressing and behaving appropriate to their rank and status. The use of "sir," "mister," initials, and formalized methods of communication were far more common. In private life, one's style tended to reflect one's grade, and wives were just as conscious of the pecking order as anyone else was.

There were fewer qualifications around, but again they seemed to command more attention, as did the possession of private wealth, connections (and titles), and an expensive education. In insurance the top jobs were reserved for actuaries; in chemical manufacturing, chemists; in engineering, engineers—although even in those days a good arts graduate or a clever accountant might move up on the outside lane.

Everyone, from the lowest to the highest, behaved with deference, and in many cases real respect, for those above them, and instructions were treated with a degree of loyalty and alacrity which may have been a hangover from the wartime (and from the difficult times before the war).

I am not looking back with a rosy view of those days. We moved, as I remember it, with much less precision than we do now. Many of those managers would be considered irresponsibly lazy or incompetent by today's standards in almost every way, but they were *managers*.

TODAY'S MANAGERS

And now, today, who are the managers? There is much to suggest that the manager is beginning to lose his or her identity. Real power is moving away from the middle and junior echelons as top management (much improved in quality and much better supplied with information and evaluations through the use of advanced techniques and electronic data processing systems) tends to make the real decisions. At the other end, the unions represent the power of organized labor, but even where no union exists, the employee, backed by recent legislation and the shortage of skilled labor, is—even in times of high unemployment—in a far stronger position than ever before.

Managers, seeing a top-management/union power axis on one hand and, on the other, a confusing array of specialists and professional staff people who also have managerial status, are moving from an old-style "manager" position to an executive gray area. Frustration and powerlessness set in, and the manager seeks to redefine himself, turning frequently to the pursuit of management charisma, a Pied Piper ability to make things go his way again, a management style geared for results.

This book offers some suggestions as to what action can be taken in different situations to maximize impact, but it may be worth considering the question of results: exactly what are we managing for? Possibly the key result is our own personal job satisfaction, but we get it through achieving results and having those results recognized as success.

VARIOUS APPROACHES

The framework in which managers are accustomed to operate is similar to that originally developed by the Romans. This is the classical line and staff approach, in which a managerial hierarchy was set up, with clear and symmetrical relationships and job descriptions and authorities at each level. In its more extreme forms, this approach is very clear and easily understood—it also facilitates movements from one position to another.

Most firms today operate a "development" of this, but they temper it with bits of the other two main approaches to organization, the human relations approach and the systems approach. The human relations approach concerns itself with creating an environment which naturally stimulates or encourages people to work together. Group technology or the ICI Weekly Staff Agreement, project teams, and participative systems are examples of this. The systems approach, on the other hand, contends that the operation of a business stems from evaluation of information. It emphasizes reporting, feedback mechanisms, and communications. Naturally, a highly developed data processing system is an essential tool in preparing the business model. Both the human relations and systems approaches are valid and necessary components of organizational design, but they militate against traditional management concepts.

PERSONAL CAREER PLANNING

So, as we put it, how does the manager behave, and how is he identified? Is there a managerial or leadership style best suited to produce results? Historically it would seem that the great pressure to obtain management positions will decrease as these appointments become fewer, less well-paid in relation to other jobs, more demanding, and less satisfying. Those who stay will need to have defined and developed skills, and the educated or ambitious will stop moving in a great mass through the various management "levels."

Initial Rules

So what do we need to do? Two initial rules may be suggested. First, to consider Einstein's statement that in an age of large-scale events and organizations, the greatest single issue of importance, apart from the question of peace or war, is for the individual to feel that he counts. You *do* matter—to your family and friends, to your company, to yourself, and to the universe. You are of significance—you *can* have some influence on events.

The other rule is, if you don't have a dream, then your dream can't come true. You can go through life reacting to circumstances, taking things as they come, but there is a danger that you may not find yourself where you had wished to be. How sad if you approach the end of your career realizing that you have abilities which have never been fully used, experiences which you have missed, and opportunities which have passed you by. Some suggestions for starting to condition and plan your career now are given here.

Suggestions for Planning Your Career

Unfortunately, we live only once. You have already lived part of your life, which leaves a balance between the present and your expected retirement date. Those precious years are all you have in order to achieve career and business objectives, and because you will spend most of your waking time in your employment, the progress of your career will be a major influence in your domestic affairs and life style. Therefore, draw a time scale for yourself, as shown in Figure 3-1. Next, visualize your retirement party or presentation. Someone who

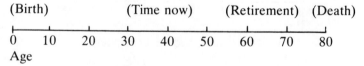

Figure 3-1. Time scale.

knows you makes a little speech. What is he likely to say about you? Consider what you would want him to say about the following things:

The position you have reached
The kind of person you are
Your relations with your colleagues
The work you have done
Your special interests

Perhaps you cannot see that far ahead, but look five, ten years into the future. Decide where you want to be and what you want to be earning. If you find your personal objectives unclear, try some self-analysis. You do not know what will happen in the future, but you know what has happened in the past. Draw an extra dimension to your time scale, as shown in Figure 3-2.

Plot in the events that have had the main emotional impact on you. These may be major happenings, such as winning a prize, doing well on an examination, getting married, finding your first job, obtaining a managerial promotion, getting fired, going bankrupt, or having a serious accident. Or they could be minor events: an argument you regretted, losing a toy, a success in the garden, a day out with the kids. Plot them in, and then perhaps rewrite the figure so that you get a clear picture. If the graph is too crowded, make two lists—the bad and the good.

Analyze the picture and see what characteristics each list, each side of your graph exhibits. What does this tell you about yourself, and how can you aim the rest of your life to have more of the satisfying experiences and less of the undesirable experiences? Having an objective—or, better still, a hierarchy or list of objectives—you can then plan how best to achieve it and over what period of time. Then you should carry out the steps listed on the next page.

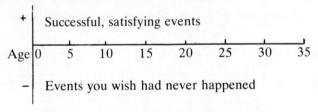

Figure 3-2. Extra dimension to time scale.

1. Let others know your aims, wherever possible and wherever tactful. This would include your wife or husband, who will be a major influence in providing moral support.

2. Find out what qualifications, experience, and knowledge will be helpful, and make a plan to acquire them.

3. Consider what friends and contacts will be appropriate.

4. Work out the steps required to put you in the most likely position to achieve your objectives and then write out formal reviews of the situation. Sit down every three months, for example, and compare where you are with where you planned to be, how it looks (are the objectives to be revised upward, downward or sideward?), and what you have done compared with what you planned to do.

You could be asking how personal career planning relates to the subject of this chapter, management and leadership styles. The answer is that until you have worked out *what* you are trying to do with yourself and *where* you are trying to go, then and only then can your style be finalized.

SUCCESSFUL MANAGERS

Leadership is tailored to circumstances, and the style for running a filing system might be inappropriate on the battlefield or in a hotel business. The sales manager, the accountant, and the factory manager all act according to their situations, but they also act according to their personalities. The two may fit very well, but many successful managers (or managers in successful situations) attribute their success to their personal style. Maybe there is a real correlation, but we all know managers who are successful despite their personal styles.

Why are managers successful (luck and ability excepted)? It is because they know what they are doing and why. They know their departmental objectives, the procedures, and the facts of the business, and they understand and are close to the people around them. They have kept their thought processes working so that they can keep on top of their jobs and ahead of the game. Crises and panics have been anticipated so that when the level of orders suddenly doubles or the computer breaks down in the middle of the payroll, there is a plan for taking the necessary action. The department is tidy and well-ordered and there are no mistakes buried under the carpet, no skeletons lurking in the cupboards. A manager who has achieved this will be confident, relaxed, objective, and approachable.

The best manager is the manager who manages best, and in general that means achieving the objectives of his function as economically as possible. We have seen and will see that management is a matter of competence and control, and consists largely in taking the right actions rather than in presenting certain styles.

Managers are human beings who work through and with other human beings. If managers in your company are expected to wear flowered ties, for example, by all means fit the company managerial image—but *be yourself.* The only way to present a consistent and understandable style over the years is to be true to your own personality. Commit your talents to the organization to whatever extent is necessary, but keep your ego and emotions to yourself.

Management, then, is about achieving results and not about particular styles. Leadership is assisted by personal qualities, but its main and indispensable component is competence.

Exercises

1. Draw your own life-span time-scale plan (as in Figure 3-1), and analyze it as suggested.
2. Determine your career objectives.
3. Write an up-to-date personal history or curriculum vitae as if you were applying for the job you eventually want. List your deficiencies and strengths in relation to your objectives.
4. Describe your own management style (as you see it).
5. List three main strengths in your style. Can these be developed, and can more use be made of them in the work in which you are involved?
6. List three main weaknesses. Do these affect the results you obtain—and, if so, is there anything you can do to overcome your problems or to prevent them from affecting your performance?
7. Analyze the style of the manager you most admire and that of the manager you least admire. Does that tell you anything about yourself? Do you dislike in others traits that you have yourself, and do you admire people who are most like you are or who would like to be like you?
8. Compare your answers to question 4 with an analysis of the style of the most successful manager you know. How would he or she act in your department?

Generalissimo Francisco Franco was in a coma for several weeks before he died. One afternoon, the coma lifted, and he heard a murmuring of many voices in the courtyard outside. "What are those people doing?" he asked his wife, who was at the bedside. "They are waiting to say goodbye," she answered. "Why?" he replied, positive to the last. "Where are they going?"

4 Personal Impact

The manager spends his day in the company of other people. They are looking at him, hearing him, and relating to him. Therefore, his personal presentation is very important.

It is easier to work with someone who is pleasant and receptive and who seems businesslike and efficient. This chapter offers some suggestions for keeping your own presentation at its best. I make no apology if some of the points seem like an insult; one has only to look around to be aware of how much room for improvement there is.

PERSONAL APPEARANCE

Are your clothes clean and well cared for? Are they appropriate to the company's style, and to the image you want to present? Are your shoes clean and in good condition? Is your hair tidy? Is the style suitable for your age and position, and does it help you to appear to your best advantage? Do you pay attention to personal hygiene?

Bearing. If you slouch, recline in your seat, and put your feet up on the desk, you can damage an otherwise good impression. Without appearing too military, move briskly and appear to mean business.

Office. Keep your office tidy. Set it up to look efficient and pleasant, to put visitors at their ease, and to make transacting business with you a comfortable proceeding. Otherwise dismal surroundings can be transformed by a good cleaning and some decorations (for example, window drapes, a picture, or a plant). A cluttered desk distracts visitors and is inefficient in itself.

Words. Words are our main medium of communication and they can do a great deal of damage. What is said once can never be unsaid. One of the rules of discussion is never to try to match other people's views, stories, or experiences unless you really can. It is better to be relatively quiet, to go away and research, and then to come back when you have something substantive to add. As a manager you will then get the reputation of always having something worthwhile to say.

As a manager, you will secure cooperation and understanding best if people like you. If they do not like you, or if they have a tendency not to like you, there will be tension that will cause them to filter out anything you say to them. In many cases, that will also lead to rejection. You must therefore have a pleasant speaking manner and say things in a likeable way. Some advice is given in this chapter, but it seems to me that some sessions in front of the company's closed circuit TV apparatus (the present-day equivalent of practicing in front of a mirror or your spouse) would be helpful.

WAYS OF SPEAKING

The speaker needs to control any internal tensions involved in the meeting. He must relax, and the way to do this is by deep controlled rhythmic breathing. Passive relaxation is where you lie down with the legs about one foort apart, the feet turned outward, the hands lying by one's side. The face in particular should be deliberately relaxed. A few minutes in this posture, breathing in for five seconds and out for ten or fifteen or more seconds, will set you up for anything. Active relaxation is when you are actually doing the talking and you relax all parts of the body other than those that are necessary for the action concerned.

Breathing is very important, and if you breathe correctly, you can carry on to the end of a sentence, however long it is. You never become hoarse, and you can go on talking even in a situation where considerable projection is necessary—for hours on end! Expand the ribcage with your abdomen in, chest out, and shoulders down. Keep the ribcage expanded, and the lungs contracted by moving the diaphragm (solar plexus) so that you breathe from the stomach.

It is necessary to get the right balance of carbon dioxide and oxygen. Shallow rapid breathing as employed by athletes (except swimmers) increases the intake of carbon dioxide; very slow deep breathing increases the proportion of oxygen and freshens the system, and this enables you to keep a clear head.

Refer back to the suggestion that you practice this type of diaphragmatic breathing, breathing in for five seconds and out more slowly—say, ten or fifteen seconds. The actor's test is to breathe out in front of a lighted candle and not cause the flame to flicker.

You must talk from the *front* of the face, that is, immediately behind the top teeth, and keep the tongue down. Say "ah" in front of a mirror and see if your tongue follows the line of the bottom of your mouth; if you find that it is stuck somewhere up above the middle, it is going to get in the way. Economize on your breathing—no big exhalations or sighs of relief. Learn to concentrate. Whenever you have a spare moment, concentrate on an object, such as an ashtray or a light fixture, and describe it in such a way that someone else would know what it is. Describe its color, form, characteristics, associations, materials, and components, and think before you speak.

USE OF WORDS

It is said that there is a correlation between vocabulary, IQ, and success. There are over 400,000 words in the complete *Oxford English Dictionary,* but the average individual uses only 3,500, although he may recognize a larger number. Some groping for the appropriate phrase or word may not matter at certain levels and on certain occasions, but in serious discussions, negotiations, and communications, it becomes important to be able to express yourself clearly and easily. Phrases like "the chairman was concerned about expenses again," "Mr. Smith said something about looking at the delivery position," "etcetera, etcetera," or "you know what I mean?" tend to come out involuntarily if one is accustomed to using them.

One suggestion is to pick out five or six words you recognize but do not use—such as from a newspaper or book—and to try to use them frequently the following week. Practice a further set the subsequent week, and the week after that, and this will gradually increase your word power. Anyone who wants to turn ordinary speaking into the true art of suggestion should equip himself with *Roget's Thesaurus, Complete Plain Words* by Sir Ernest Gowers, and H. W. Fowler's *Dictionary of Modern English Usage* (edited by Sir Ernest Gowers), and a good old-fashioned dictionary.

As stated, then, speak with a hard palate and a hard stomach. You cannot breathe through your nose when you are talking. This means that if the atmosphere is smoky or otherwise polluted, you deny yourself the filtering activities of the nose. If you have to do a lot of talking, do not spend the previous evening talking in a polluted atmosphere. Furthermore, when you are talking, relax and open the back of your throat. This will save undue wear and tear on your vocal chords.

VOICE INTEREST

Making your voice interesting and attractive comes under the following categories: phrasing, pauses, pitch, pace, inflection, stress, emphasis, and volume. These should all be varied to provide interest, but what is needed here is to use the rules mentioned thus far (and, of course, substantial preparation), so that your mind will be clear to concentrate on the effect of what you are saying and on how it is being received by the listener. Prepared or partially prepared talks need a great deal of rehearsal, although when they are given as an after-dinner speech or a lecture, they may appear completely spontaneous. The same approach should be applied to meetings, where one may have to make proposals or responses, which can be known or guessed at beforehand. Where matters arise for which you are not prepared, it may be better to avoid trying to answer completely on that occasion.

A word is necessary about dialects. Dialects and particular speech characteristics may be musical and attractive, but their most common effect is to make it more difficult for other people to understand you if your accent is different from their own. Furthermore, you may not pronounce certain sounds too clearly. Practice these sounds, along with your enunciation and potential tongue twisters, for a few minutes as you drive to work.

EFFECTIVE LISTENING

It is just as important to listen effectively as it is to speak effectively. Here are a few ground rules:

1. Concentrate fully at all times, and make a real habit of paying careful attention, even if it appears that the speaker either is saying something you have heard before or is talking rubbish.

2. Interrupt as little as possible; let people finish what they are going to say. Their view on when to stop may be different from yours, and you may create considerable frustration and misunderstanding if you do not allow them to finish.

3. Have an open mind and deliberately obliterate your own prejudices. This is particularly important when talking to people very much younger or older than yourself, where the effect of being brought up in a different period leads to different attitudes.

4. Use empathy; put yourself in the other people's shoes and try to analyze what they are driving at, what they are feeling, and what they want to communicate. Respond by nods, smiles, and positive facial gestures, so that they will be encouraged to think you are receiving their message.

5. Care for, appear to care for, and acknowledge points of view other than your own. As you know from experience, life is very seldom black and white. It is quite possible to draw different conclusions—all with some validity—from the same facts and analyses.

6. We should always attempt to respond intelligently and to help the speaker get his points over clearly, even if we are going to differ from him subsequently. We are all tempted to give someone a hard time every once in a while, destroying arguments by wit and sarcasm and other less elegant devices, but this should be avoided.

A well-managed plant is a quiet place; a factory that is "dramatic," a factory in which the epic of industry is unfolded before the visitor's eyes, is poorly managed. A well-managed factory is boring. Nothing exciting happens in it because the crises have been anticipated and been converted into routine.

PETER F. DRUCKER

5 Objectives

Very early in this book we mentioned F. W. Taylor's three prerequisites of control: the necessity to know what one should be doing, how one should be doing it, and how long it should take. Much sorrow and uncertainty will come to the manager who does not know exactly what he is doing or how much of it he should do and in what amount of time. The manager should have personal objectives, as well as company or departmental objectives. It is very difficult to have a full sense of achievement if you do not know what you are attempting to achieve. It is also difficult to attempt to achieve things that you believe to be impossible. The old adage, "the impossible we do at once; miracles take a little longer," is excellent as a statement of intent, but as a task for everyday living, it has some shortcomings.

MANAGEMENT BY OBJECTIVES (MBO)

The technique of Management by Objectives is one in which the organization states its clear overall targets and then works out plans, both functionally and for each individual, whereby those plans can be achieved and whereby the achievement of them is monitored by routine reviews. It suits the style of some chief executives and the organizations to which they belong to operate in this controlled and ordered fashion, but it requires a great deal of effort to proceed in this way. The majority of readers of this book will not be in organizations where forward moves are planned or proceed to plan, but are more likely to be in a more flexible or dynamic situation. This is not to say that flexibility and dynamism are impossible under MBO; very much the reverse: what we are really saying is that most readers will be from companies where MBO is not in operation.

One of the fundamental needs of people is the security of knowing where they stand and what they are trying to do. This is particularly true of the manager who is responsible for human and material resources other than himself. To retain his sanity and to make best use of the resources he has available, he must be quite clear as to what he is trying to do, how to do it, and, as was said before, how much time he has.

DEFINITION OF OBJECTIVE

An objective must be specific, it must be achievable, and it must be desirable. Let us quote an example. You are house services manager, and part of your operation includes the mailroom. The *function* of the mailroom is to deliver the mail; the *aim* of the mailroom is to deliver the mail as quickly as possible; the *objective* of the mailroom might be to deliver the mail by nine o'clock each morning. That is a very simple statement of an objective and it may of course be argued that it is impossible to deliver the mail by that time without increasing the staff of the mailroom in an uneconomic manner. It is quite permissible to modify the objective and to deliver the incoming mail by 9:00 A.M. nine days out of ten and by 9:30 A.M. on all occasions. Let us look at that. The objective is specific there, the question of whether it is achievable or not has to be considered, and the question of desirability should also be considered. It may be that nine o'clock is the time by which the mail is required and that, therefore, to deliver the mail prior to nine o'clock would not be appropriate. To close down the mailroom entirely and to use the premises as, for example, a bingo hall, might be very much more profitable; but again, it might not be desirable.

STANDARDS OR TARGETS

Under the heading of objectives, we are really talking of a number of standards or targets. It is sometimes said that an individual middle manager cannot really make objectives that affect the company; the company policy, whether on a fully or partly planned basis, is made by others, and the manager has to react to the situation as it arises. The more he is able to control his own department or his own function, the better he will be able to react to changes and also to contribute to the company for which he is working.

Most managers have this basic need or compulsion to accept responsibility, which is why they are managers. They also need to understand fully their own areas of responsibility and how well they are performing. To do this, managers must learn to think in quantified terms. The CEO has to think in quantified terms, translate these figures onto paper, and plan to achieve these results.

Overall Objectives

Profits do not just happen; they result only if objectives are being achieved in a range of areas, and these are likely to be achieved only if the managing director has done his part. The chief executive and the chairman of the board have to consider important matters, such as what the company is really in business for and what its objectives are in the short, medium, and long term. Whether or not they have done this, the individual manager still has to find targets or standards of operation for his own function.

In many cases, the manager, whether he be on a departmental, branch, divisional, or section level, is closest to the customer and to the actual work going on; he is in the thick of the action. The manager is often better qualified than senior management to know what the customer is likely to accept, what the staff is likely to do, and what is practical in particular circumstances. He may well be the best person to recommend objectives or to propose what is feasible in his own area to fit in with an overall company plan, or, as is suggested in this chapter, to run his own operation or function to the best satisfaction of himself and of the company.

Individual Manager

We mentioned some overall organizational objectives, but for the individual manager his targets or standards are going to fall under two headings. First of all, these will relate to the business and will be operational standards; the second group relates to the staff and resources which are under his control. The functional or operational standards fall under the following headings:

Cost
Income or turnover
Quantity
Speed
Quality
Errors
Service
Company image
Risks

Some of these overlap and some will apply in combination, but the second group of objectives, which may be ancillary to the foregoing, include:

Training
Development
Promotion and succession
Staff turnover
Staff changes
Up- or downgrading of work
Restructuring

Objectives are not equally important. The manager should consider whether these headings are relevant to his own function, and he should rank them in order of priority so that he and his subordinates devote their major efforts and skills to achieving the most valuable results. It is not easy to give a comprehensive set of example objectives, because in every area the circumstances will be different. It is suggested, however, that it will be easiest in the first instance if the objectives are listed and if the following four additional columns are drawn in beside them. An example of this is given in Figure 5-1.

Objective	Action to be taken	Responsibility of	Controls	Review date
(examples) 1. To select and train deputy by 10/1/81	Prepare job specifications. Ask Personnel Dept. to advertise internally and externally. Make sure John Smith applies.	Manager	Advertisements placed. First interviews Final selection Man in post Training completed.	2/14/81 4/1/81 5/1/81 7/1/81 10/1/81
2. To increase turnover by 15% by 12/31/81	Circulate 100 largest customers once a month, drawing attention to best buys, and follow by phone calls within 3 days.	Manager – 2 senior sales assistants.	Letters to be posted by end of first week in month Review turnover in 3 months to see if increase obtained. Replan if results not satisfactory.	8/8/81 9/5/81 10/7/81 9/23/81
3. To reduce invoicing errors to not more than 5 per month by November 1981.	Record errors daily and post on wall chart.	Senior asst.	Examine chart every Friday and discuss with staff. Review progress.	10/31/81
	Carry out 10% spot check on invoice calculations.	Senior asst.	Reduce to 5% when objective achieved. Review 3 months later.	10/31/81
	Train junior invoice clerk in procedures.	Manager	Junior clerk to be proficient by	7/29/81
	Ask O & M Dept. to suggest a clearer invoice layout, and advise on an additional calculator.	Manager	Proposals to be received by	7/29/81

Figure 5-1. Objectives action plan (specimen).

Objective. Whichever heading it is under, this first column must be specific, achievable, and, of course, desirable. Under some headings such as company image, it may be difficult to be specific, but there is still good reason to attempt this—such as the proportion of people knowing the name of the company, or the number of disparaging complaints received in a given period.

Action to be taken. In the second column will be put the means of the proposed plan of achieving the objective. In the case of the example of the company image, this may result in redesigning the letter head, or altering the layout of the shop window, or spending $5,000 on advertising in the trade press.

Responsibility of . . . In column three, the actual person who is responsible for carrying out the action specified in the previous column is entered. In many cases this may be yourself. In other cases it would be somebody under your control.

Controls. This column indicates the means by which you will know when you have achieved, or are in the process of achieving, your objective. For example, how does one know when one's company image has improved to the extent that 10 percent of the population knows the name of the company or that 5 percent knows the name of the company and what it makes? In that rather unusual case, perhaps one would be carrying out a sample investigation of the population at large four times a year, and if this reveals the appropriate level of recall, then the initial objective would have been achieved.

Review date. The fifth column is either the date by which you wish to have achieved the objective, or the date at which you apply the examinations or the controls to see what progress has been made before determining a further control or review date.

Systematic and Disciplined Approach

Much of this type of exercise is done unconsciously by managers in their everyday life. However, as we have seen before, a systematic and disciplined approach covers not only areas that have been missed but also areas that otherwise would have been swept under the carpet because they were difficult to deal with. If the manager gets into the habit of thinking of his personal and departmental objectives in specific terms and in concrete dates and plans for achieving them, then he will begin to achieve considerably more, and will be achieving it in a more reliable, satisfying, and comprehensive way.

Exercises

1. List three objectives under different headings for your own area, and rank them in order of importance.
2. Prepare an objectives action plan to deal with those three objectives.
3. Determine if there are any of the items on the list of standards which are in no way applicable to your function, and state why.

PART
II

MANAGING OTHERS

A plan is a list of actions arranged in whatever sequence is thought likely to achieve an objective.

JOHN ARGENTI

6 Planning and Scheduling

PROVIDING A SERVICE

Whether your function is one of the major areas of direct action such as sales, production, and accounts, or a supporting role such as personnel or records, you will be providing a service. This service may be to customers or other outside organizations, or it may be to other internal departments, but whichever it is, your job and prospects depend on its being performed in an efficient, competent, and acceptable manner.

Your job is to make a sufficiently good estimate of the likely demands on your department or branch so that you can arrange to have the manpower, materials, equipment, and other facilities available to meet these requirements. This chapter looks at some simple methods of forecasting or estimating the likely incidence of demand, and of adjusting manpower resources to meet those peaks and troughs.

For example, in Britain, when one is attempting to forecast the behavior of soccer teams in order to set up betting pools, the first step is to remove the "bankers," teams that are most likely to win or to lose, because entering these on the coupon will reduce the number of teams that have to be considered in detail. The same applies to planning. There are certain things that are known, such as the weekly payroll; it happens every week. Other things are also known—for example, that Christmas will be on December 25 every year. These are perhaps very simple examples, but there are certain things in every business which can be known very well in advance.

SEQUENCE AND TIMING OF OPERATIONS

Planning and scheduling are concerned with the sequence and timing of operations. This will range from "deciding the priorities" to batching and allocating specific parcels of work to be done to a timetable. The information the manager needs will likewise range from the very general, such as a general feeling as to how long one can leave an item before trouble may arise, to detailed work contents of individual procedures, estimates or counts of volumes, timetables of requirements by other departments, customers, and data processing, and plans of staff availability and commitments such as holidays, day-release, and courses.

Listing the Work and Applying Two Concepts

Let us start by listing the work in our particular area. This will be variable, but it will include all the activities performed, for example, booking orders, processing claims, logging work orders, filing copy letters, training, personnel activities, maintenance, inventories, and so on, depending on your function. The second step is to apply two concepts to these specific items of work that we have pulled out.

Concept one. One is that of splitting work up into three distinct parts: first, preparation or make-ready; second, the job or operation itself; and third, the completion phase, which may be putting it away or following up afterward. Let us give an example concerned with a meeting. The preparation phase is the issue of invitations, circulation of agenda and papers, arranging the room and administration, and any briefing activities. The second, or operation phase, is the actual meeting, and the completion phase is preparation and circulation of minutes, review of action to be taken, filing away papers, and so on.

Over and over again, this three-stage concept applies. We get out pen and paper, we write, then put away the pen and paper. We set the table and prepare a meal, we eat it, then we wash up and put away the dishes and cutlery. Within each sequence are other sequences. For example, when doing the dishes, we get the dirty things, fill the sink, get the dish-washing liquid as a preparation phase, then we actually wash up, followed by the completion phase of emptying the sink, drying the dishes, and putting them away.

Concept two. The second concept which we can apply is to divide the work into three other categories: first, controllable or fixed work; second, semi-controllable or semi-fixed work; and third, variable or uncontrollable work. By uncontrollable or controllable, we mean the degree of freedom we have over its sequence and timing. (For example, the entry of customers into a branch is bound to be variable or uncontrollable in our definition.) When we have finished this separation, we will find that there is work which has to be done every day, week, month, or year, whether we like it or not, and also that there is work which comes in on a more sporadic and unexpected basis. However, we can divide the latter work into preparation, operation, and completion, and in some cases the preparation can be done at our own discretion and the completion can also be done at our convenience.

You will see that by doing this we are isolating our bankers (to use the example quoted earlier), the things that we know and can control, leaving at the bottom of the list those things that we do not know and therefore cannot control. The proportion of the variable work compared with the rest will vary from business to business, but let us say, for the sake of argument, that it is 50 percent. In other words, half the work is composed of routine or expected work, which is subject to normal managerial controls and a certain amount of discretion. The other half is dependent on external influences, such as the weather and the political and economic situation. This 50 percent of variable work can then be subdivided into the three categories of preparation, job, and completion, and a further proportion of it can therefore be regarded as controllable. One is gradually narrowing down the amount of work to which estimating procedures need to be applied. The best way of estimating the future is to know what has happened in the past: the method of doing this is going to vary from business to business but these notes are suggesting some simple kinds of planning and scheduling frameworks that may be of assistance.

SIMPLE TYPES OF FRAMEWORKS

Volume of Input

A typical starting point might be to assess the likely volume of input to the department (such as orders, enquiries, and so on). This can be recorded over a period to enable an estimate of the future to be reached, or it may be an informed guess on the basis of knowledge of the business or the plans of other departments. A simple presentation might be like the one shown in Figure 6-1. Another way is to try putting the graph the other way around and to note the difference, as shown in Figure 6-2.

Conclusions could be drawn from this pattern, but let us look at another situation—Figure 6-3.

Which is it easier to estimate the future pattern from, Figure 6-3 or Figure 6-4? The figures are the same in each case.

But consider the first example with a different scale, as shown in Figure 6-5. Again the same figures, but it is easier to read.

Moving Averages

Another way is to use "moving averages." Most volumes and frequencies fluctuate and it may be better to graph the average of the orders of the last four weeks (or last three months, and so on) each week to get a more reliable picture of the trend (for example, as shown in Figure 6-6).

Would you have made the same forecast from each of the last two graphs? Figures can be made to prove anything, and it is important to look at your method of forecasting to see that it is the most appropriate one to show the pattern of business.

The longer a graph or tabulation is kept, as a general rule, the more reliably one can forecast from it. To offer again a simple example, see Figure 6-7.

On this particular example, one could plot in, perhaps as a dotted or colored line, the forecast for the year, and then continue to plot the actual figures, seeing whether they are as expected—or, if not, whether some of the assumptions one made have changed, and what the implications may be in this and other respects.

Orders received. Week commencing:

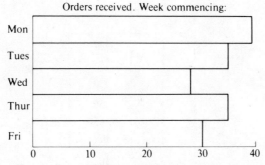

Figure 6-1. "Orders received" graph (1).

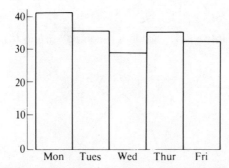

Figure 6-2. "Orders received" graph (2).

Orders received per week commencing:

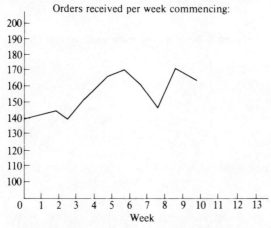

Figure 6-3. "Orders received" graph (3).

Orders per week

Week	No.
1	140
2	145
3	150
4	155
5	165
6	157
7	162
8	146
9	170
10	164

Figure 6-4. "Orders received" graph (4).

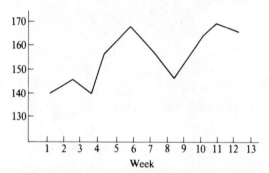

Week

Figure 6-5. "Orders received" graph (5).

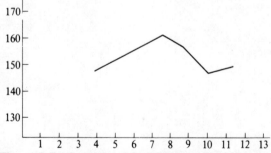

Figure 6-6. Average orders per week on a moving
four-weekly basis (1).

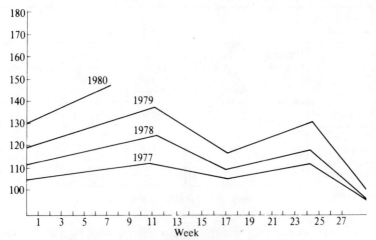

Figure 6-7. Average orders per week on a moving four-weekly basis (2).

Events or Tasks

Another type of planning is not concerned with volumes or frequencies; it may relate to events or tasks, such as:

21 December	Christmas lunch
5 January	Children's party
6 January	Long-service-award presentation
9 January	Staff committee meeting
12 January	Sales managers' conference

or

Write to old customers X, Y, & Z Inc.
Investigate volume of complaints concerning packaging.
Design and place advertisement for new sales assistant.
Prepare sales report for Mr. A. (by 31st January).
Arrange for car to be serviced. Replace front shock absorbers.

Simple schedules of this kind can be noted in a diary or in a file that can be consulted every day. (Never rely on your memory!)

They can also be tabulated: consider the training matrix, as shown in Figure 6-8.

Here, "T" indicates that the person concerned is trained or experienced in the function specified. It would show what cover there is for sickness and holidays, or what would happen if staff leave or are transferred, or again how the section might be able to cope with increases of work in one area or another.

Section personnel	Section tasks				
	Vetting orders	Pricing orders	Preparing plant instructions	Preparing weekly sales figures	Customer complaints
Mr. Goodone	T	T	T		T
Mr. Winner	T	T		T	
Mr. Sitter	T	T			
Miss Fitt			T		
Miss Take		T			
Miss Handle					

Figure 6-8. Training matrix.

A chart like this can be turned into a training plan by deciding who needs to be trained or cross-trained in what and writing down a sequence of training to be taken up on a programmed basis, or whenever the work load drops.

Multiple Activity Chart

Much of the foregoing can be used in a fairly general way, but for more detailed planning or scheduling a multiple activity chart may be the answer. Two examples with different degrees of details are shown in Figures 6-9 and 6-10.

These particular charts are very simple and show little more than the sequence of operations and interaction of persons. The work will vary each day, so the time blocks are determined by the latest completion points for each activity. Given an assessment of the work content, this can then be done more precisely.

Sample Loading Charts

The times given in Figure 6-11 and Figure 6-12 are for example only.

The load can be programmed into the multiple activity chart or on to a loading table.

Loading Table

It may be questioned whether, in a small section, it is worth going to this detail or whether an exercise of this type should be done regularly.

Time	Mr. A	Miss B	Miss C
9	Read management figures	Open mail	File yesterday's copies
10	Attend management meeting	Take minutes	Obtain files for day
11	Read mail	Draft minutes	Calculate weekly sales figures
12	Dictate answers	Receive dictation	
1	LUNCH	LUNCH	LUNCH
2	Check minutes	Type letters	Check and type figures
3	Draft	Type letters	Make duplicate copies
4	Check and sign	Type minutes	Mark copies for distribution
5	Interview new employee	Prepare outgoing mail	Distribute copies

Figure 6-9. Multiple activity chart (1).

Staff	Monday		Tuesday		Wednesday	
	Present	Tasks	Present	Tasks	Present	Tasks
Mr A	X	Budget return Figures for prize points scheme	X	Check stocks of sales literature Lunch with Sales Manager, M N O, Ltd.	X	Reorganize window display
Miss B	X	Prepare envelopes from customer mailing list	X	Complete envelopes		(Dentist, 10:00 A.M.) Prepare payroll
Miss C	(Day off)	—	X	Stamp brochures	X	Sort out stationery cupboard

Figure 6-10. Multiple activity chart (2).

Job	Basis of assessment	Time (mins)	No. Current backlog		Workload
Vetting orders	per 20 orders	30	60	20	2 hours
Pricing orders	per 20 orders	60	40	180	11 hours
Works instructions	per set	10	36	—	6 hours
Sales figures	per set	420	—	—	—
Customer complaints	per each	16	24	93	31¼ hours

Figure 6-11. Loading chart (1).

Job	Basis of assessment	Time (mins)	No. Est.	Act.	No. b'log	Workload Hrs.	Mins
Counter tour bookings	This time last year + 10%	25	14			5	50
Written tour bookings	This time last year + 10%	10	2		4	1	00
Counter tour inquiries	2 inquiries per booking (current experience)	7	28			2	16
Written tour enquiries and brochure requests	Last year + 15%	15	4		8	3	00
Rail ticket sales and inquiries	Per 10 tickets sold	90	50			7	30
Business house work	Estimated	180	—			3	00
Customer complaints	6 per day	20	6			2	00
Payroll preparation	Constant	60	1			1	00
Addressing envelopes	Per 15 addressed	60	100			6	40

Figure 6-12. Loading chart (2).

Day	Miss D			Miss E			Miss F		
	Work in	Load hours •	Work done	Work in	Load hours	Work done	Work in	Load hours	Work out
Typing itineraries	100	5		100	5				
		4	20		4	20			
		3½	10		3	20			
		2	30		2	20			
	40	4		30	3½				
Typing invoices				30	4½		180	6	
								2	120
									60

Figure 6-13. Loading table (1).

This is a matter for individual managers, but it should always be considered as a factual proposition. Is 15–30 minutes a day spent on detailed planning by the manager worth, say, a 10 percent increase in effectiveness (3 persons × 10 percent of 7 hours = 2.1 hours a day), and will he be able to ensure a more efficient and reliable operation by doing it? Figures 6-13 and 6-14 show examples of loading tables.

Tables of this sort can be extended, of course, to show the position of the work and of the staff at any time. They can be used to plan the

Day	Miss D			Miss E			Miss F		
	Batches in	Load hours	Batches out	Batches in	Load hours	Batches out	Batches in	Load hours	Batches out
Vetting orders	10	5		10	5				
		4	2		4	2			
		3½	1		3	2			
		2	3		2	2			
	4	4		3	3½				
Pricing orders				1	4½		6	6	
								2	4
								—	2

Figure 6-14. Loading table (2).

work and its completion, and schedule its performance among the staff. This method can be taken further to see how expected rather than actual work loads could be planned for, when work would be completed, and when problems of over- or underloading and specialist cover would arise.

MANAGING PEAK LOADS

The principles of managing peak loads are explained here with the help of diagrams.

The Condition

When the capacity to handle work is less than the work load in a period, there is a peak load.

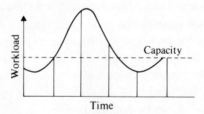

There is a shortfall between the time available to do the work and the time required to do it.

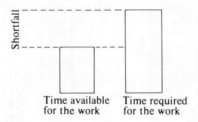

The Aim

We have to manage (i.e., set objectives, plan, organize, control, motivate, and innovate) so that the peak condition is eliminated, or much reduced.

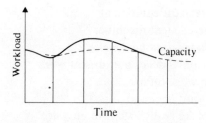

We have to find ways to minimize the shortfall between time available and time required.

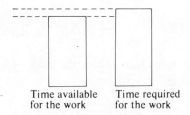

Time available   Time required
for the work   for the work

The Options

The things we can do to balance work capacity and work load in the peak period fall into three groups.

1. *Increase the time available.*
   Work shifts on machines
   Work overtime
   Employ temporary staff
   Combine two sections
   Postpone routine servicing of equipment
   Reduce interruptions, e.g., queries

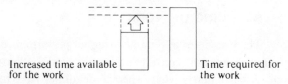

Increased time available   Time required for
for the work   the work

2. *Decrease the time required for the work.*
   Simplify methods
   Motivate—ask for extra effort
   Temporarily eliminate some steps, e.g., checks
   Temporarily reorganize duties/layout, e.g., flowline

Borrow/hire extra equipment

Install more efficient machines

3. *Decrease the work to be done.*

Select priorities—delay non-urgent work

Reschedule work inflow

Send work out

Perform "make ready" steps in advance

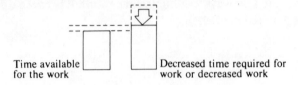

Time available
for the work
Decreased time required for
work or decreased work

The effect of such actions is to reduce the peak by:

Cutting off its top

Taking from its base

Minimize the peaks' effect by increasing the capacity to handle work.

The Solution

Each peak load problem can be solved with a positive approach which draws from these options.

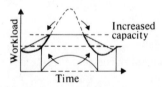

BATCHING OF WORK

The principles of obtaining higher performance through "batching" of work are now considered. Issuing work in "batches" facilitates control, particularly where specific deadlines have to be met. A reasonable run at an activity is more satisfying to employees and, if they are allowed to concentrate, they work up to a much higher speed. The preparation and completion phases are reduced in relation to the operation, and the employee settles in to the task.

In batching of work, the following principles will be found helpful:

1. Batches should, where possible, start and finish with the natural breaks in the working day.
2. Batches should be composed of work suited to the skill level of the particular recipient.
3. Where possible, batches should be alternated to provide variety.
4. As a rule, the smaller the batch, the more sensitive the control of the situation.
5. Batches that are too small should be sized according to the preference of the recipient. Some people prefer fairly short batches; others work best with a long, steady run.
6. The recipient should know when the batch issued is due for completion.
7. Overruns in batch duration in excess of, say, 15 percent should be investigated, and corrective action taken.

Remember that reasonable pressure of work is good for morale and motivation. Very large amounts of work tend to overwhelm and demoralize staff, but very small quantities may be ignored until the last minute, unless there is good feedback and control. By scheduling, an objective or plan can be understood by all in terms of direct action. Also by scheduling, good organization and allocation of work is achieved.

Exercises

1. List the functions or activities of your department.
2. Are there any major figures or incidents that determine the level of activity? Can the volume and occurrence of these be estimated, or are there any historical records to suggest a pattern?
3. Have you any method of work measurement or assessment? If not, how do you work out the correct staffing for present and future loads?
4. Are there any activities to which the following techniques could be applied?
   Graphical records or tabulations of quantities
   Diary-type planning
   Matrix planning
   Multiple-activity charting
   Loading charts
   Batching controls
5. Isolate your peaks and troughs and consider whether you could use any of the suggestions made in this chapter.
6. Construct a training matrix or grid for your department.

Yet a little sleep, a little slumber . . . so shall thy poverty come. PROVERBS 24:33–34

7   The Decision-Making Process

All our working life we are concerned with making decisions. Even at a very early stage we are involved in them, such as deciding whether to approach the boss; whether to do A before B; whether to try to sell a customer the $100 set or the $150 set; whether to take a check or insist on cash; or whether to apply for a vacancy. At the very top, the chairman of a large company is still making decisions, such as whether to buy another company or to proceed into a new market, or to clinch a particular deal.

At home, again there is a series of big decisions such as, should we have another child, or buy a new car or a bigger house? There are also small decisions: shall we decorate the guest room this week, or shall we leave it until next year? Shall we plant onions again this year when they did so badly last year, or shall we go for some more potatoes?

All these decisions have one thing in common: we are never in possession of all the facts on which to evaluate them thoroughly—in other words, to prove the point conclusively. If we were able to do that, then perhaps the need for making the decision would be of a different quality. However, when we are not able to prove the point, but must make a decision on a balance of probabilities or estimates or guesses, then we are very much dependent on another quality—decisiveness. This is the capacity to make up our minds and decide to take action, and then to take that action, when we are *not* in possession of all the facts.

At one end of the spectrum, we have people who will make a decision or take action when they have no facts at all or practically no facts. We would call these people reckless. At the other end of the spectrum, we have people who will continue calling for further facts and doing further investigations without reaching a decision at all. Or there are those people who keep changing their minds. I am sure that all of us have worked with people who come to a conclusion one day and then rethink the matter the following day and come to a different conclusion. Who is to say they are wrong? But then action, which is the lifeblood of business, is not taken perhaps when it should be. In addition, the staff people who have been looking to us for a lead find it very frustrating if we keep changing our minds. If they have to adjust to new policies too frequently, they will come to the conclusion that perhaps we do not know what we are doing.

I am sure you will have all seen by now that decisiveness comes with confidence, and confidence comes with knowing what we are doing, or at least *thinking* that we know what we are doing.

In this chapter, we offer a simple system for disciplining the mind—the subject of decision making—and also one or two techniques for assisting in evaluating one course of action as opposed to another.

MECHANICS OF DECISION MAKING

These basic processes are illustrated in Figure 7-1, and consist of:

Define the problem
Examine the facts
Consider the alternatives
Include the views of others
Decide the course of action
Evaluate the results

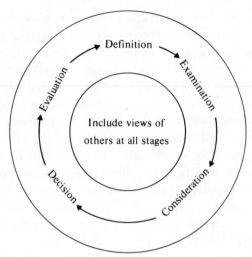

Figure 7-1.

Define the Problem

This is so obvious that it hardly needs saying, and because it is hardly ever said, it is frequently overlooked. By defining the problem, one often defines the answer. A manager, pestered by a lot of simple questions from his people, got them to put them in writing. Much to his surprise, he found that many were never brought to him because when people defined the query sufficiently to write it down, the answer became apparent to them. Problems are often expressed in vague terms, such as "runaway inflation," "ecological suicide," and "military confrontation," which have emotive overtones, and suggest a disaster situation. Since the situation is a disaster, we decide there is nothing we can do about it, and the decision-making process moves from solving the problem to avoiding it. However, if we know we must budget for, say, a 25 percent increase in costs, or that we have 50 years left to develop an alternative to fossil fuels, then we will have defined the problem better, and, in so doing, pointed to the action to be taken to solve it.

A problem often encountered is the need for more sales (or presumably to make more profit from existing business), but how much more sales? If the problem can be defined (for example, to make the required return, we need x dollars more income), then we can begin to consider how those sales can be secured. It may be that y dollars more of a product or service needs to be sold; but, in any case, you will be in a better position to start the decision-making process. Always be as clear as possible on what the problem is before you start on any important decision-making process. Be aware of what really is the matter.

Examine the Facts

Write down what facts you know about the problem and what facts you do not know. With respect to the latter, consider how much effort or how much expense it will require to obtain these facts and to determine the likely accuracy of these facts once you obtain them. You can also go to a great deal of effort to obtain facts that are of doubtful validity to your solution of the problem.

Consider the Alternatives

This is very important. With an open mind, you should consider all the possible courses of action which can be taken. Many people who have let their minds wander through either a personal brainstorm or a brainstorming session that can be conducted with others and have thereby thought of "stupid" alternative ways of doing things, have often stumbled on quite important ways of doing things to better advantage.

Include the Views of Others

This is noted here as the fourth step because it fits the fourth letter of the mnemonic DECIDE. However, it is complementary to all other steps in the decision process. Including the views of others is important for two reasons. First, others may think of ideas which you have not considered yourself, or may be in possession of information which you do not already have. The other reason, particularly in the branch, is that if your staff people feel that they have participated in decisions made in the branch, they will be more willing to identify themselves with the action that has to be taken as a result of those decisions.

Decide the Course of Action

The decision is made by balancing quantified advantages and profits—and unquantified advantages and benefits—against quantified costs and disadvantages, and against unquantified costs and disadvantages. Obviously, the closer these are to each other, the more difficult the decision will be to make. Some methods of evaluation are offered later in this chapter.

Evaluate the Results

If we have made the right decision, justified by subsequent events, we should consider why we made that decision and whether the same line of thinking or line of action would lead us to make the right decision again. If we have made the wrong decision, have we made the wrong decision for the right reasons, or have we made the wrong decision because we have pursued an unsatisfactory decision-making process or lacked certain important facts? Unless we do this evaluation after our decisions, we may in fact find ourselves making the same mistake over and over again, or, perhaps even worse, making the right decision several times and then making a disastrous mistake because we are not aware exactly of what we are doing.

FACTORS IN EVALUATION

Ranking

This is the simplest form of evaluation, in which we decide that X is better than Y and Y is better than Z, and so we can set out our list of alternatives or priorities, in order of their importance.

Weighting

This is a step further than ranking, in which we say that $X = 10$, $Y = 5$, $Z = 0$, and so on. In other words, some factors have more importance than others. For example, we are to choose a branch manager for an insurance company, and we decide that we are going to make our choice on the basis of five factors: technical knowledge, managerial skill, personal relations, maturity, and seniority. We decide that technical knowledge of the business is most important, and give it a value of 10. Managerial skill is important, but less important than insurance knowledge, so we give it a rating of 7. Personal relations are very important, but not quite as important as the others, so we give them a rating of 6. Seniority is important in our company, and we give it a rating of 3, whereas maturity is similar to seniority but slightly more important, and we rank it as a 4.

You will see now that we have ranked the various qualities which we think a manager of our particular branch should have, but we have gone one step further and have applied weighted ratings to them because some characteristics are more important than others. These particular ratings and rankings may not be applicable to your company, but they are given as examples nevertheless.

The next step in using these factors is to add them all together, and you will see that in this case it comes to a total of 30. We would then divide by 30 each particular factor (for example, 10 for insurance knowledge) and come up with a decimal result (see Table 7-1). In the case of insurance knowledge, it would be .333; managerial skill, .233; personal relations, .200; maturity, .133; and seniority, .100.

Finally, the various applicants are interviewed for the branch manager's position, and each one is rated against the various factors which you have chosen, on a scale of 1 to 10. At the end of the interviews, we then multiply by the decimal factor the various scores for each man or woman, as the case may be, and we complete a weighted score or corrected score for each person interviewed. This will not automatically make the choice for us of our new branch manager, but it will help us make a better quality decision through thinking about the subject in a disciplined way, and, where the choice between one person and another is narrow, it will help us make the decision on a more rational basis.

DESIRABILITY AND PROBABILITY

It is very important for us to select the right branch manager, but if we have picked the wrong man, there are a number of ac-

Table 7-1. Specimen table showing use of weighting.

Rank	Quality	Weight	Factor	Candidate A		Candidate B		Candidate C	
				Raw Score	Weighted Score	Raw Score	Weighted Score	Raw Score	Weighted Score
1	Insurance knowledge	10	.333	6	2.000	9	3.000	4	1.332
2	Managerial skill	7	.233	7	1.631	5	1.165	7	1.631
3	Personal relations	6	.200	7	1.400	5	1.000	10	2.000
4	Maturity	4	.133	9	1.200	8	1.065	10	1.330
5	Seniority	3	.100	8	.800	10	1.000	6	.600
	Total	30	1.000	37	7.031	37	7.230	37	6.893

Factor = Weight divided by total of weights
Raw Score = Rating on a scale of 1 to 10
Weighted Score = Raw Score multiplied by Factor

tions we can take to mitigate the effects of our bad decision: we can dismiss him, transfer him, train him, or supervise him. So there we have a very important but not an irrevocable decision.

If we back a horse in a race for $2, we are making a different kind of decision, because once the bet has been placed, it cannot be canceled—the horse either wins or loses. If we are a little less decisive, we may back it to show or place. But once the race has been won or lost, there is nothing we can do about the result. If we lose $2 by backing the wrong horse, it is not terribly important; but had we been backing it with a month's wages, for example, the decision would have caused certain tensions inside us and it would have been an important, even irrevocable, decision. If we had such a decision to make, we would probably have refrained from making it. The probability of a horse's winning would have had to be very high for us to take such a risk.

This introduces the question of desirability and probability. The *desirability* of our having a big win on a race track is very high; the *probability* of our doing so in that particular case is low. In our earlier step of defining the problem, we probably determined the desirable characteristics of a successful decision in the particular project on which we were engaged. In many business decisions, this characteristic is profit, and if we apply the probability of the occurrence of certain aspects of our evaluation, we will then have another dimension in our decision making. Let us take an example.

Suppose that you are proposing to operate a holiday center on a certain island in the Mediterranean. First of all, you estimate your likely business in this holiday center, and you would then rank the various possible levels of booking. Let us say that for 1981 these would be 24, 75, 125, 175, and 225 (flights). A big variation, but in practice, of course, the project could be a great success or fall flat on its face (although by your actions you would have some measure of control over what would happen). The next stage is to put a probability factor against each of those booking levels. This is very similar to the weighting of importance which we applied to the various characteristics we were seeking in our branch manager. In the case of probability, the maximum probability is 100 percent. Therefore, one must divide 100 percent between the various levels of bookings in their probability. For the sake of this example, let us say that we take 12 or .12 as the likelihood of making up 25 or 225 flights, we get 23 as the probability of 75

Table 7-2. Example calculation: Bookings on XYZ island— proposed vacation center.

Booking levels	25	75	125	175	225	
Probability factor	.12	.23	.30	.23	.12	
	Gross profits at booking levels (000)					
Alternatives:						
1. Convert existing hotel	$350	$1,080	$1,800	$1,800	$1,800	
2. Build new hotel	$340	$1,080	$1,800	$2,500	$2,500	
3. Do both	$320	$1,050	$1,780	$2,500	$3,200	
	Profitability converted by probability factors (000)					Gross expectation (000)
Alternative 1	$42	$248	$540	$414	$216	$1,460
Alternative 2	$40	$248	$540	$575	$200	$1,603
Alternative 3	$39	$242	$534	$575	$384	$1,774

and 175, and 30 as the probability of 125. We are saying, in fact, that we are most likely to reach a medium point on the bookings, but we are not certain that that is going to be the case. (See Table 7-2.)

Let us set these out and consider what we should do. On the island there is an existing hotel which is in a poor state of maintenance, and we have the choice of converting the existing hotel, building a new hotel, or, in fact, doing both. There are many considerations to be applied, but in terms of profit our accountant has worked out what would happen.

One sees the gross profits likely at each different level of booking, and then, by converting the gross profits to probabilities through multiplication with our probability factors, we come to the second set of figures which shows our gross expectation. You will see that at $1,774, we have the greatest potential profit in building the new hotel and also in converting the existing hotel. Again, this kind of mechanism may not make our decision for us, but it will put us in a much better position to evaluate the alternatives and it will be easier to make our profit budgeting for that and the following year.

Without the benefit of analytical tools, the human mind tends to make decisions in two ways. A problem occurs and the mind looks at its memory and says, "Where have I seen a problem like that before, and how was it solved?" The second thing that the mind tends to do is to stop once the needle in the haystack has been found, whereas it may be better policy to look through the entire haystack to see how many more needles there are, and then make a choice of the best one!

Exercises

1. What decisions do you regularly make? List six of them, and describe what method you use to make them. Are any of them "win/lose," that is, irrevocable decisions?
2. What was the biggest decision you have ever made? How did you make it, and was it successful?
3. List three decisions that could be made by using ranking.
4. List three decisions where simple ranking would be improved by weighting.
5. List three decisions where the use of probabilities would be significant.
6. Have you ever avoided making a decision or felt like avoiding one? Are there any decisions you would avoid now?
7. Are there any circumstances where it is better to stick to a bad decision than to reverse it? Give an example.
8. What factors would contribute most to improved decision making in your company?

Definition of a committee: the unqualified drawn from those unwilling to consider the unnecessary.

8   Meetings and Reports

MEETINGS

It is sometimes said that the best meeting is a committee of three with two absent. Meetings may be held for the purpose of disseminating or collecting information, or for communicating decisions, but the meeting we are talking about here is where several interested parties sit down and work through an agenda, either planned or spontaneous, discussing each subject in turn and arriving at conclusions for action.

Necessity and Purpose

The first thing to do is to decide exactly what the meeting is expected to achieve and whether this is reasonable. Perhaps the next thing is to decide whether to hold or attend the meeting at all. Time is being spent with a number of managers, and you should consider whether the cost is going to be commensurate with the result. Are we ready to hold a meeting, and are you ready to play your part in it? One cannot be axiomatic about this, but I try never to attend any meeting for which I am not properly prepared or briefed. If you find yourself discussing unexpected items on the agenda, or you are in areas where you haven't done your homework, you will waste valuable time in the meeting, and you may find yourself having to adopt a negative approach because you have not done your own thinking in advance.

Therefore, prepare yourself, and make sure that you know what the meeting is for; estimate what you think is its likely result. And, if this is good for you, it is good for the other people who should be invited: they must be given an opportunity to read any necessary papers in advance and know what is likely to come up for decisions. You would also work out their likely personal objectives and the probable course of their personal approach (and also your own). Consider who can usefully contribute to and gain from the meeting, but there are others who should be advised for political or status reasons. Perhaps if you keep them informed, they will not actually need to attend.

Preparation

Get to the meeting before it starts. I do not mean merely be on time. (And how much time is wasted by people sitting around waiting for the chairman or other members to arrive?) This is the question of getting used to the surroundings of the meeting and laying out your papers so that you can concentrate fully when the meeting starts. To further this, the good secretary will see that the administration does not intrude and that there are sufficient chairs, tables, paper, and pencils and that coffee and tea, if appropriate, have been ordered.

During the Meeting

When the meeting starts, the chairman should not assume automatically that all members realize what the meeting is for; he should state its purpose clearly. No advantage is gained by making the meeting last any longer than is required for achieving these purposes. The cost in salaries of those attending the meeting can be substantial, and their presence there often means that departmental and other decisions are delayed until they return to their posts. Committees become little groups in their own right, and time is spent on matters that have no relation to the objectives of the enterprise.

If you are making proposals, always explain them in terms of what effect they will have on the others who are listening, and consider why those people should be interested in listening to what you have to say, if at all. You must listen to the arguments of others and be patient with their objections. Very often, people are content to have the opportunity to state an objection, and, having let off steam, they will allow matters to proceed. In real life there are very few proposals which receive immediate and unanimous approval, if they have been given any proper consideration. (Some suggestions as to how to present proposals in the most favorable light are covered in Chapter 10.)

In meetings, remember to "take the temperature." You should learn to study the expressions on the faces of those around the table and notice what they are doing. For example, they may be sitting back with their arms folded in an expression of withdrawal, or leaning forward, tensed up with something they might like to say. They may be nodding with approval or frowning with anxiety. If the mood is one of acceptance, then, of course, a decision can be reached and recorded. If the decision seems to be going against what you want, and if this matters, stop that decision from being made. You can easily say that there are more facts to be gathered or analyses to be done, or that this was a preliminary proposal, or you can defer it in some other way. Once a "no" decision has been made, it is much more difficult to reverse.

Eventually you will have made your points or proposals and the meeting will be moving to a conclusion. If the conclusion is the one you want, this is fine, although one's colleagues do not always like to see too much manifest success. Whatever conclusion the meeting reaches (even if that is only to continue the discussion at the next meeting), it should be specifically agreed upon and, if minutes are taken, recorded, before going on to the next item. Where action is determined, it helps to put the name or initials of the person concerned against the minute and to declare some time for review or completion. For example, compare "it was decided that the production department should review the situation concerning excessive scrap" with "Mr. Smith, the production director, agreed to submit a report on scrap percentages by May 17 and circulate it to the members of the meeting."

Reviewing the Situation

There should obviously be some mechanism for reviewing action taken on decisions by any meeting, and the composition and frequency of the meeting should also be down for review at regular intervals. Many businesses have regular meetings which are little more than just shop talk. Another fact to consider is how long people can concentrate and stay awake at a meeting. There are meetings which go on for hours and hours, and everyone concerned feels very heroic when they stagger back to their homes late in the evening. But while they were at the meetings they were either unobtainable in their departments or else were subject to a series of disturbing interruptions during the meeting. One suggestion is to decide how long the meeting should take and keep to these guidelines so that other arrangements can be planned around the meeting.

Summary—Meetings

1. Determine the objective of the meeting.
2. Prepare yourself; plan the tactics and timetable.
3. Decide who should attend.
4. Advise the participants in time for them to prepare.
5. Have all necessary papers ready, and circulate them to others who need to see them in advance.
6. Arrange accommodation and administrative details.
7. Start the meeting on time.
8. State the purposes of the meeting.
9. Direct the discussion, stage by stage.
10. Take the temperature of the meeting. Always keep in mind the objectives and feelings of the participants.
11. Agree upon specific conclusions at each stage.
12. Nominate people responsible for action and for review.
13. Arrange the time and date of the next meeting (if required).

REPORTS

In management literature, meetings and reports seem generally to be linked, presumably because often a report is either called for by a meeting or is presented to a meeting. This may be the best way of dealing with the situation, but the manager will consider whether by calling a meeting of this kind, he is spreading the risk rather than allowing the person responsible to make the decision on his own.

There are two distinct phases in constructing a report. The first is to marshal all necessary information; the second is to read this information in the way most conducive to the right decision or action being taken.

Marshaling Necessary Information

As a minimum, you must have answers to these questions:

1. What is the real problem? What specific illustrations can you give of the real problem? What is the report meant to say?

2. What is the answer to the problem? Does the report give the answer or enable the recipient to form a satisfactory conclusion? Again, can you provide specific illustrations?

3. Why should the recipient be interested in the answers? What benefits will it provide? Again, be specific in defining the benefits or results. Benefits that cannot be quantified become a matter of subjective opinion.

4. If results and benefits are involved, state clearly how much these will cost in various forms of resources and how long it will take to achieve them.

The marshaling exercise consists of writing down every relevant fact, proposal, or conclusion—preferably on separate pieces of paper, so that they can be sorted into a logical sequence during the second stage.

Framework of the Report

In planning the arrangement of a report, two approaches can be taken. One is that where there is a standard company form, it may be better to follow it, since the recipient will be familiar with it. However, where there is no standard form or where the standard form seems inappropriate, the arrangement should follow a form which satisfies the reader's priority of interest. Normally you state the results first and then discuss how you arrive at them. A form which normally satisfies this and is widely used is the summary or précis report, which covers the following points:

Objective or purpose
Scope or summary
Conclusions
Recommendations

Body of the Report

Objective or purpose. The purpose of doing a summary report, which should seldom be more than two or three pages long, is to orient the mind of the reader and to make it possible for those who don't want to question the conclusions to ascertain what they are, without having to wade through all the supporting details.

Scope or summary. Reports should always have a title and a date and indicate to whom they are addressed and by whom they were prepared. The report should contain an index or contents page showing what it contains and where it can be found. The summary or précis report should follow; the précis commences with a statement of the objectives of the report, why it was commissioned, who asked for it, and when. The scope or summary briefly indicates the resources and method employed so as to give an indication of the depth of the conclusions and to draw attention to any special features of the work. But like the previous paragraph, this should not be more than two or three lines in the normal way.

Conclusions. These should follow the conclusions or findings. This should be done in tabular form, and in a series of positive statements. For example:

1. That a reduction in wastage of 3 percent could be obtained by. . . .
2. That orders could be processed through the office in 24 hours if. . . .
3. That an additional assistant manager in the export section be appointed with effect from. . . .
4. That the reason for the accident was the. . . .

Recommendations. The final part of the summary is the recommendations, and this is a list of specific actions to be taken following the conclusions. For example:

1. That the factory manager be authorized to obtain tenders for a new grinding machine with the object of having it installed by. . . .
2. That the revised method of order processing be installed by the office manager on _____ and that the organization and methods department be requested to assist in the installation.
3. That the personnel manager be asked to proceed with the recruitment for the new assistant manager position.
4. That the committee's findings be forwarded by the secretary to the appropriate government agency.

Writing the Report

Most people have no need to be involved in any systematic writing or literary effort after leaving school or college. Therefore, the manager who finds himself needing to write a substantial report or letter may find it a difficult exercise. He may make the report too brief and sketchy, or long and tedious, or may evade it altogether and try to get by with a verbal proposal. Indeed, a verbal proposal may be a very good way of obtaining approval, but all managers will need to write some important proposal, report, or letter at some stage.

To be persuasive, writing needs a disciplined approach and repeated polishing. Good writing skills cannot be acquired overnight; they cannot be won through a formula, and it is also unlikely that without regular use writing ability will remain at a satisfactory level. There are, however, some guidelines that will give you a better prospect of success.

Include testimonials or illustrations. Here are several examples: "similar equipment was installed in the ABC and the XYZ company last year and has given satisfactory performance"; "this type of training has produced remarkable results in the invoice department—three operators increased output by 25 percent within two weeks following the course"; "the scope for obtaining savings through methods improvements is substantial (for instance, the replacement of typed addressing on envelopes by the use of window envelopes has saved 150 hours of typing each month)"; and "the problems facing the division cannot be compared too closely with those confronting the other areas of the company. However, in a competitive company, MNO Inc., there was a somewhat similar situation when. . . ."

Use linking words in your writing. Linking words help the reader follow your thinking, and they are most important in opening paragraphs. Examples of such words are:

next	meanwhile
besides	remaining
then	the result
alternatively	in contrast
previously	in total
equally	in some
nor	yet
so	final
also	first
similarly	second
specifically	third

Next time you read anything by a successful author or writer, see whether these linking words have been used to carry your attention from one point to another.

Use headings and subheadings wisely. Chapter headings and subheadings attract more readers than the body of the report does. If they are persuasive, these lines will help sell the reader; if they convey little, they lessen reader interest. The test here is which headline or heading conveys the information most persuasively or clearly. As an example, judge for yourself which heading should go on a paragraph: "benefits" or "financial benefits for company staff." Try this one: "findings" or "your principal problem areas." Short, dry headings (for example, "distribution report by Mr. Smith") may be succinct, but "opportunities for reducing distribution costs in the XYZ warehouse" may attract more interest.

March your readers through your subheadings. That sounds like a difficult task, but if you use frequent subheadings—say, every 200 or 250 words—you will help your readers along. They know from the heading what is coming up in the next sentences. These reinforce the subheadings and, therefore, you make your good points twice over. As with headings, so with subheadings: a single word may count for nothing. "Resources" conveys little, but "additional staff resources for the textile division" would surely merit closer attention.

Use "power" words. Some words add power to headlines and sub-headings. Consider using them when appropriate. These words include:

important	remarkable
improvement	announcing
quick	fear
advice	loss
how to	win
introducing	first

Avoid long words, sentences, and paragraphs. The jargon words of technical specialists and the ponderous phrases of self-styled orators tend to drive readers elsewhere. Use short, plain English words, and in your first draft write sentences of between 10 and 20 words. If you want to add style, this should be done in the final draft of the report. Try to restrict your paragraphs to eight lines or under. Use active verbs to give force and drive to what you have to say. For example, "we installed a computer" (active) instead of "the computer was installed by us" (passive).

Cut excessive verbiage. It depends on what you are writing, but, as suggested earlier, you should initially write down everything that comprises the work done to produce the report. As a second step, you should cut out everything that is really not relevant. Such trimming—and many letters and reports could be cut by one third—can rarely be done at the time of the first draft; it takes place in the editing or polishing stage. It is very difficult for a writer to edit his own writing, since he knows what he meant to say. If you can get a colleague to read and comment, he may point out that the sentence that was quite clear to you could convey another meaning to someone else, or it could appear confused. Most people have a rather subjective impression of their own ideas and views, and in any case, if you have spent some time in compiling the report or letter, a fresh approach may well be of value.

Get right to the point. When giving recommendations or conclusions, do not lead into them with a number of lines; state them simply, as follows: "The recommendations are: 1. . . . , 2. . . . , 3. . . . ." Do the same with any other results or statements. Make your points quickly and save your readers time. If you want to expand, do so after your first enumeration, by saying: "the following facts support those recommendations," or "more detailed information follows."

Tabulate paragraphs. For a series of unrelated facts or progressive paragraphs, a useful device is to number them sequentially. Do not string disconnected thoughts together in long slabs of type.

Avoid overuse of capitals. DO NOT USE LARGE NUMBERS OF CAPITALS. PEOPLE READ ALL THEIR BOOKS, NEWSPAPERS, AND MAGAZINES IN LOWER CASE. This applies also to the reports, tables, and contents page. The reader's first impression is of strangeness when a lot of capitals are used: he does not write in capitals, so why should you?

Avoid negatives. The use of negatives confuses people, and turns what should be simple into something which is too complex. For example: "This is not to say that additional training would be unwarranted in all circumstances, nor that it could not be positively beneficial in certain cases." The writer of that complex sentence could just as easily have said, "Additional training may be beneficial in certain cases."

Avoid bull. Take, for example, the following statement: "I am absolutely convinced that the proposals would be the best thing that ever happened to the department, and the equipment proposed is the most advanced available in the world today." This sort of statement overemphasizes the point and leads to resistance on the part of the reader; in any case, it adds very little to the content of the report. Another important point here: *Avoid stating the obvious!*

Summarize. This final point is one of the most important of all. Summarize your main idea in three or four sentences at the opening of each report or chapter or each main section of your letter. Summaries are probably best written in some distinctive way at the beginning of the section to which they refer, but you may summarize at the beginning of the letter or report, at the end of it, within individual chapters, or in a covering letter, if there is one. You do not want to confuse the reader by using different literary tricks, but it may be valuable in stressing what you want to say to summarize at any appropriate point in the report.

To sum up the main points of good writing:
1. Include testimonals or illustrations.
2. Use linking words.

3. Use headings and subheadings wisely.
4. March your readers through your subheadings.
5. Use "power" words.
6. Avoid long words, sentences, and paragraphs.
7. Cut excessive verbiage.
8. Get right to the point.
9. Tabulate paragraphs.
10. Avoid overuse of capitals.
11. Avoid negatives.
12. Avoid bull, and avoid stating the obvious.
13. Summarize.

Exercises

Meetings

1. Prepare an agenda for a meeting at which the various meetings held in your organization will be reviewed. List the meetings involved, the attendance, and the appropriate duration.
2. Imagine that the meeting has taken place and that you have had your way in all respects. Draft minutes to record the decisions taken.
3. Imagine that the board has decided to relocate in a development area 150 miles away. You have to announce this to the senior executives at a meeting. Prepare a plan of how to put the decision over most effectively and consider how you would deal with any likely objections or queries.

Reports and Letters

4. Write a newspaper article of not more than 500 words, illustrating your present job or project.
5. Examine your last major letter or report, and criticize it in light of the points made in this chapter. Would you have written it any differently now, and in what way?
6. Draft a short report addressed to your chief executive outlining the three weakest aspects of your organization and proposing the necessary action and restructuring required.
7. Write an application letter for a better position showing why you should be given serious consideration for it.

If you are not contributing to the solution of the prob-
lem, then you are part of the problem yourself.

CHINESE PROVERB

9 Motivation

Let us first try to define what we mean by motivation. Consider one situation: you bound up your garden path after work, throw open the front door, and give your wife a big hug. "I had a wonderful day at the office, dear—I got so much done," you say to her. "I did this, I did that, I got this approved, I finished that," and so you go on all evening telling her about the wonderful events of the day. This continues until you suddenly realize it is half past ten, and you suggest an early night so that you will be fresh for the meeting tomorrow morning. Needless to say, you bound out of bed at dawn the following day and rush into work with your head full of plans.

Contrast that with the following situation: you drag yourself up the front path, fumble with the lock, and sink into the big chair. "Get me a drink, dear," you gasp, "and make it a stiff one. I'm just about wiped out. I've had a hellish day at the office. I got absolutely nothing done."

Most practicing managers live their lives on a more even keel than veering between those two extremes of feeling, and perhaps it is better that they do so. However, work occupies the major part of our waking time and energies as managers and employees for perhaps 50 years of our lives, assuming that most people start at about 18 and retire in their late sixties. There must be an enormous difference in terms of productivity and creativity (apart from personal values) between living those 50 years as a pleasurable and exciting activity and suffering through them as drudgery. If the difference were as little as 10 percent (and most experienced managers know that it is considerably greater than this), it would be the equivalent of working another five years during one's career.

DIFFERENT APPROACHES

The manager has to decide how motivated he wants his employees to be. There may be some occupations where a relatively static frame of mind is better because there is little demand or opportunity in the position. Certain security and reception positions might fall into this category. But other jobs require motivated people. This chapter suggests a number of approaches that can be tried to stimulate your idle and apathetic subordinates. First of all, here are some basic points.

Children

When we are young, we are very dependent on others, especially our parents. If those "significant others" satisfy the child's needs and make him feel secure and loved, then when he grows up his attitudes are more likely to be secure and dependent, socially inclined, and associated with people, because he is used to people satisfying his needs.

If a child does not know where he stands and cannot exert influence over his environment, he will become insecure (fearful) and aggressive (hostile) and will seek independence. He will concentrate on personal (egoistic) needs, developing ways and means (such as power, control, money, and the acquisition of material things) by which he can obtain the independence he desires.

If the child wants independence and cannot get it, he will retreat into fantasy. If you (child) do not get what you want, you react aggressively. How do the parents react? Submit or counterattack? Probably they get the child to repress his aggressive feelings, so there is often tumult under a calm exterior.

In fact we do suppress our feelings, and our outward appearance may not reflect what is happening inside—and what happens inside is different for different people. Not everyone views the world from the same perspective as you do.

People We Know

When we know people well, such as relatives or close friends, we do not always understand exactly what happens inside their minds, but we know pretty well how they will behave in a variety of situations. We know how they will react to what we say and do, because we have seen them reacting in the past. This applies also to groups of people we have come to know, such as the customers, the staff, the head office, our bosses, and so on, and this is fine, as long as we do not assume that because people are behaving in a particular way, they have a similar feeling about what they are doing and why they are doing it.

People We Do Not Know as Well

The problem arises when dealing with people one does not know so well, such as new customers or new members of staff, or where a novel situation arises, or where people start to react in an unexpected or contradictory way. It is in dealing with such situations that the manager proves himself, but first of all he must start by understanding himself.

Let us take an example. The owner of your company, Mr. Smith, has been trying to get the business of a certain large firm for years. He seems at last to be succeeding and has been asked to meet its CEO next Tuesday afternoon at 4:00 P.M. He asks you to accompany him and to prepare a write-up on the company to be used at the meeting. This seems to be recognition for you, and naturally you want to do well at the meeting—particularly since you are an assistant branch manager and one of the managers at another branch may be leaving shortly.

You work all weekend and, with the help of your own manager, you produce a marvelous folder and write-up to bring to the meeting. You are to meet Mr. Smith outside the customer's premises just before the appointed time. Naturally you arrive early, at 3:30 P.M., and wait. At 4:00 P.M., he has not arrived, so you go into the reception area. He is not there, and eventually you decide to go in yourself, but the receptionist tells you that there is no appointment arranged for Mr. Smith or yourself; she allows you to telephone back to your company, but Mr. Smith's secretary says that he went on a trip to Bermuda two days ago, and didn't he tell you?

Reactions

How do you feel at that point? How do you react to the situation? Three types of reactions are possible:

1. Angry—directed against Mr. Smith or a more generalized disgust with the company or your job.
2. Disappointed and humiliated. Do you feel ashamed or doubtful about yourself?
3. Rational—for example, "I wonder why he didn't tell me?" "What should I do next?"

Most people would feel some of each type of reaction, but we can be reasonably sure about which would predominate.

Mr. A has been successful at school and in his private life; he did well in his last job and he has good and easy relationships within the company. Mr. B has not found life so easy and has just scraped through. He is not well known in the company and has had some uneasy encounters in his time.

How will A and B react? Self-confident Mr. A will be surprised and frustrated by this check to his progress and will probably be angry with the obstacle and those responsible for it. Mr. B, who is pessimistic about his abilities but would nevertheless like to be successful, may react differently. He may vent his anger inwardly and perhaps use the incident as further proof of his own inadequacy or his stupidity in taking on the job or task. In other words, a series of failures can lead a man to the conclusion that he can be no longer certain that the world has gone wrong; perhaps it is *himself* that is lacking something.

Mr. C's reaction—the purely rational one—is more rare. He is the man who feels no emotional upset at all, any more than dropping a coin on the floor or forgetting his handkerchief. It is a problem, but not worth getting excited about.

How does the perspective of Mr. C differ from that of Mr. A or Mr. B? (I am not talking here of *apparent* reactions, but of real ones.) It is a situation in which A's and B's needs for status and self-esteem are challenged. Mr. C, however, lives in a wider and more secure world in which his esteem needs have been satisfied many times and he can see a variety of methods of achieving his aims—and, possibly, a variety of aims. Both A and B could mature into C, and if they do, they will be less likely to encounter obstacles that now seem serious (for them), and will be less likely to blow up if they do encounter them.

However, in business life, if one does meet an obstacle which leads to very angry feelings, it is bad form to get very angry about it. You must show a controlled and rational facade. Inside your blood pressure is rising, and there may well be physical side effects in due course. (An occasional blow-off would be a healthy thing.)

But the ideal executive is the one who does not get frustrated in the first place, such as Mr. C, who simply shrugs his shoulders at himself and the world and starts to think where to go from there. His self-esteem is so solid that few things could threaten it. His ego needs are for accomplishment of organizational goals—achievement and self-actualization.

People's Expectations

What is the problem? It is people's expectations about their ability to satisfy their needs, and their expectations are effectively determined by past successes and failures.

If, through life, one has come to expect failure and to feel unsure of one's ability to satisfy one's personal egoistic needs, then these needs loom larger than they do for another person. The American psychologist H. J. Leavitt gives an example of a badly mixed drink: is it just a badly mixed drink or a sign of disrespect from the barman? It depends on the outlook of the person who's drinking it.

People like Mr. B will be less rational about their efforts to satisfy their needs, and it follows that you should build up people's feelings of self confidence. Let us turn to success and failure, since experience of both has such a major effect.

Success and Failure

Mrs. A and Mrs. B are of equal ability. Mrs. B thinks a salary of $20,000 a year means success, whereas Mrs. A thinks that $25,000 a year means making money. Both earn $22,500 per annum, but which thinks she is a failure?

There is a relationship between our aspirations and our ability to achieve them. The closer they are, the better; excess either way creates frustration. People develop different attitudes, even from an early age. Take an example. As a counter clerk, you are on an incentive scheme. The first month of the scheme, your sales are $10,000. You have worked hard, but you aim for $15,000 sales the following month. (In most situations in life, we tend to set goals slightly ahead of our present abilities or performance.)

But suppose another counter clerk, younger than you, gets $18,000 sales in a month. What is your target then, and how would you feel about selling only $15,000?

Once other people enter into the target-setting process, the more or less natural tendency to set targets a little ahead or related to past achievement breaks down. At that point, targets may be set without any regard to ability. In business or industrial life, standards are accepted or imposed which are inappropriate to the individual's inclinations or abilities, resulting in frustration (or refusal to accept). Frustration arises where failure to surmount an obstacle threatens one's personal well-being.

Self-confidence is tied to success, and success is in large part how other people define it.

Conflict of Goals

Another problem is where goals conflict with each other—such as opposing needs for dependence and independence—particularly where the conflict relates to internal conscience needs. Remember that repressing feelings burns up a lot of energy.

Let's take an example. You are assistant to Mr. X, a very decent, hard-working man. He has helped you a lot and you are good friends. He has been in his position for a long time and desperately wants a promotion. He has a large family and has a bit of a struggle to make ends meet. The CEO calls you in and offers you the job of Mr. X's boss, Mr. Y, who is moving up. You ask about Mr. X, but the CEO says that you have more ability and potential than Mr. X. He says that he will have a word with Mr. X, but that although Mr. X is good at his job, he might not be as good in a more senior position, whereas he thinks you will be. You obviously take the job, but are you feeling delighted or guilty or both? Perhaps you have some worries about it. What do you say to Mr. X after he has seen the CEO?

The answer to that question is quite important. This is an extreme example, but there will be many occasions when you are participating in a situation which is bad news for somebody else. If both you and the other person are hardened "Mr. C" types, then perhaps there is no problem, but bad news can be hard to handle. Mr. X would find it very difficult to avoid making some remarks that you might both regret later, and you would find it hard to conceal your delight at getting the job he wanted.

Mr. X was very close to tears as he walked down the corridor, and you were the last person he wanted to see. However, he soon gets his feelings under control, at least on the surface. By the following morning, just as your elation wears off, he has rationalized the situation: the senior job involved risks; he would be away from home more; the extra money after taxes was not worth it; he feels in a better position with you in the hot seat; and so on. He has psychologically dried his eyes, and you can meet him without tension.

Sometimes unpleasant decisions are announced in the middle of meetings. Decorum prevents immediate protest from those affected by the decisions, and by the end of the meeting there has been a considerable measure of adjustment to the new situation. The human mind works quickly, but emotions often get in the way, and take much more time to adjust.

Summary

To sum up, the successful manager must work to understand his staff and customers as people. He must put himself in their shoes and try to appreciate their feelings. Once he has moved toward this understanding, he will find them much easier to work with—people respond to those who understand them. People also respond to situations that give them what they want. Self-fulfillment, success, and freedom are all subjective matters, and therefore it is up to the manager to help others see these as positive parts of their environment.

CHANGE AND JOB SATISFACTION

The examples of the motivated man who had done so much and of the frustrated man who has achieved nothing have just been given. The research of American psychologists such as Maslow and Herzberg has suggested that the major factors in motivation at work are contained in the work itself. These factors include achievement; recognition; the actual suitability and congeniality of the work itself; and associated matters, such as opportunities for responsibility, promotion, or acquisition of skills. The demotivators or features that cause frustration and discontent are principally poor (or misunderstood) policies and administration, and bad relationships with one's managers and colleagues. The question of leadership styles for motivation and results in different situations is discussed in Chapter 3, but this section looks at the psychology of change and how to structure more motivation or satisfaction into work when making changes.

In this context, increased job satisfaction breaks down into six rules:

1. Allocate work in natural units or complete transactions.
2. Increase individual responsibility and authority (job freedom).
3. Reduce routine checks and controls.
4. Issue management control figures and reports directly to those concerned.
5. Introduce new tasks and challenges.
6. Agree on specific areas of expertise.

Allocate Work in Natural Units or Complete Transactions

People feel that their work is more important and valid if they handle a complete module. For example: "I look after all of our business in New Jersey"; "I deal with x kinds of policies from start to finish"; "I am the link between production control and the rest of the works"; "I do the entire assembly and then pack the widgets for shipping."

Increase Individual Responsibility and Authority (Freedom)

Wherever possible, let people assume full responsibility for the correctness and quality of their work. Let them be responsible for reports or letters produced by them or for clearing work ready for other departments or work stations. Discretion over pricing rates, refunds, granting of credit, special arrangements, or small differences in sequence and method can often be granted—to a greater or lesser degree—to responsible junior staff people in whom you have confidence. The effect of this kind of authority is to broaden the individual concerned and to enable him to demonstrate his potential. Freedom (whether used or not) is a valuable and valued job advantage.

Reduce Routine Checks and Controls

By removing some controls, we do not mean to reduce accountability. Where mistakes are correctable, unlikely, or of minor significance, checking can be reduced to sample proportions, but employees who feel they are trusted with something of importance will rise to the responsibility and feel a sense of personal achievement.

Issue Management Control Figures and Reports Directly to Those Concerned

Staff people are motivated by measuring the results of their work and their achievements against objective standards, agreed-upon targets, or the requirements of the situation. It is a courtesy and indication of recognition to let them have "their" results directly and in no way lessens the authority of management and its need to interpret and control.

It is sometimes argued that to pass on sophisticated information (such as a company's annual report) to junior personnel is a waste of time and paper, but staff people (who in some cases are tomorrow's managers) and their families are becoming more widely educated. Given a chance to take a more intelligent interest in the affairs of the organization, some at least will begin to do so. Even if the figures are not fully understood, the courtesy in distributing them will be appreciated, and the "we are never told anything" syndrome will be reduced or avoided.

Introduce New Tasks and Challenges

This is so obvious that it is often overlooked, since most people operate at a far higher level of interest and concentration if they are being challenged or stretched (reasonably!) and are given the stimulus of being trained and developed for new tasks. Problems can arise when change is feared or when salary and job-grading considerations have been allowed to become barriers to flexibility rather than a system for fair reward.

Agree on Specific Areas of Expertise

This rule follows logically from the last. It is not intended for one to create a cadre of indispensable specialists with "little black books" of exclusive information. What is suggested is that where expertise is required (for example, in legislation, export-import formalities, taxation rules, routings, and client details), individuals can be given specific areas in which they can become conversant. As the individual becomes an expert on one subject, he feels more important and is proud of his position. The subjects themselves become better known in the group, and staff people know where to turn for help on technical or special matters.

Exercises

1. Describe yourself through the eyes of your main subordinate. Would he or she be irritated, frustrated, or disappointed by any of your traits or actions and by what would be seen as your strong points?
2. Describe yourself as seen through the eyes of your boss. Are there any ways in which you could appear to better advantage or be understood more fully?
3. List your subordinates and, next to their names, list their main likes or motivations, and their main dislikes or demotivating influences. Do you know them well enough to be reasonably sure you are right?
4. List six main causes of frustration in the department and six causes of job satisfaction—excluding five o'clock and payday!
5. Apply the "six rules" mentioned here to the work of your department or office, and decide on at least one improvement for each job position.

By long forebearing is a prince persuaded.

PROVERBS 25:15

10 Persuasion and Selling

This chapter is elementary, and it covers rules and precepts which almost everyone reading it will know. Selling and persuading are not very complex activities, but why do we fail so frequently to apply the correct procedures? It must be true that any manager requires a certain minimal command of the arts of persuasion for his own use, and sufficient understanding of them to be able to teach and counsel others.

BASIC POINTS

If I go to a butcher shop and ask for a pound of sausages, the young assistant "sells" me the sausages. He receives my order and processes it to my satisfaction—that is, to the point where I have paid for the sausages and left the shop with them wrapped up at the bottom of my shopping bag.

These are very important tasks, but suppose the assistant says, "All right, sir, a pound of sausages, and we've just had a delivery of some first-class bacon. Look at how fresh and moist it is. . . ." Here, the assistant is creating a very different situation. He is starting to sell me some bacon, but what he is doing appears not to be the same as what he did when he sold me the sausages.

However, in both cases the decision is mine, the buyer's. In the first case, I identified my need for the sausages, whereas in the second it is the assistant who identified my "need" for the bacon. Of course, I may not "need" the bacon because I simply do not like bacon; or I have just bought some elsewhere; or I do not like wise-guy assistants to push bacon at me; or I may not have enough money to buy the bacon, however much I may want it; or I may always buy my bacon from the supermarket; and so on. In this case the assistant has wasted his time (and mine), and it is now more difficult for him to say, "And we have some lovely eggs," than it would be if you had liked the bacon.

KEY FACTORS IN SELLING

You may object and say that housewives do not shop like that any longer, but these simple examples illustrate some of the key factors in selling:

1. Selling is creating an opportunity for the buyer to buy.
2. Buyers only buy if they fell they need to.
3. Buyers can only buy if they have the money.
4. Buyers prefer to buy from someone they like and trust.
5. Buyers like to see what they are getting.
6. Buyers like to feel they are getting good value.

Could we rephrase those points and look at them from a managerial aspect—the implementation of change, for example? Change is more acceptable:

1. When it is understood than when it is not. (Explain the reasons, objectives, and mechanics of the change.)

2. When it does not seem to threaten security than when it does. (Explain what effects the change will have on the person and his job, the future, and the organizational structure.)

3. When those affected have helped to create it than when it has been externally imposed. (Wherever feasible, develop new methods and procedures, in consultation with those who will be affected.)

4. When it is implemented after prior change has been assimilated

than when it is implemented during the adjustment to other major changes. (After each major change, allow for an adjustment period.)

5. When it follows a series of successful changes than when it follows a series of failures. (If several changes over a period of time have failed to solve a problem, it may be better to avoid any further change for a while.)

6. When those affected can see a positive advantage in it. (Explain the benefits of the change, such as better distribution of work load, more responsibility, better use of talent, and more opportunity for training.)

7. When it results from an application of accepted policies or principles than when it is dictated by personal order. (Avoid major change that results only from your personal likes and dislikes.)

8. To people new on a job than to people old on the job. (The more oldtimers are affected by the change, the more important it is to apply other principles listed.)

9. When the outcome is reasonably certain. (Where the outcome is uncertain, try the change on an experimental basis for a limited time period, for a test area, on a selected number of products. Set up a schedule for follow-up.)

10. If the organization has been trained to plan for improvement than if the organization is accustomed to static procedures. (As a manager, encourage suggestions, develop a questioning attitude, establish an understanding that failure of some ideas is considered part of the cost of progress. Where there is no "freedom to fail," people will seek the safe—rather than the best—solution.)

Final Decision

As we saw, buyers or subordinates prefer to buy from someone they like and trust, but no matter how much power a boss may have, no matter how superior he may be, it is his subordinate who controls the final decision in any change or instruction. It is the employee who ultimately decides to come to work or stay at home; the child decides whether to obey or not. The boss can threaten or persuade, but in the end he is dependent on the subordinate. It is the boss who is motivated, it is he who feels the tension and whose needs are unfulfilled.

The boss represents only one force acting on the employee—he never has complete control. The employee has infinite techniques for evading or defying changes imposed by his superior.

Criticism. Employees who expect to be criticized whenever they are not working may learn to *act* busy (and also when not to act busy), and that the boss is an enemy. They are provided with a challenging game to play against the boss: who can think up the best ways of loafing without getting caught?

Frustration and aggression. He knows, too, that change or conflict may lead to frustration and hence to aggression or disturbance of some kind. Such a reaction is normal and the boss should not always take this as a sign that he has failed or has gone too far. A good idea is to get the subordinate to take the responsibility for understanding the boss, the situation, and the handling of the change (for example, getting the student to feel he is responsible for his education rather than the teacher, or at least that the responsibility is shared). The boss may also be advised to understand why he acts the way he does, and what his motives are.

Method of Presenting Choices

One point which must be stressed is that there is a method of presenting choices, proposals, and decisions which is likely to be faster and more successful than other ways. Whether it is the salesman selling bacon or a director persuading fellow members of the board, or a manager talking to his subordinate, certain key precepts must be observed.

People are not computers; they have logical minds, but they are also a mixture of feelings, ambitions, frustrations, hopes, and fears. They interpret logical proposals logically, but their logic is colored by these feelings and emotions, whether they know it or not.

The answer is to present every proposal first in terms of the effect (benefit or advantage) that it will have on the individual himself: "There is a way in which you can avoid all this searching of the case papers"; "this change will enable you to get away on time"; "this new car means that you can drive for long distances without strain." Then follow the benefit by some illustration, visual, or physical effect that will stimulate his interest, such as charts, photographs, models, drawings, flipcharts, blackboards, mock-up forms, or graphs. If possible, get him to handle it or try it, and thus involve some or all of his senses.

Only when you get to the point you have identified do you go into the necessary details. Remember, too, that he may not be interested in how hard you worked to produce it, where it came from, and other data. This may be vital to you, but what is vital to the buyer is what affects him as an individual.

CREATING THE BUYING SITUATION

I do not advocate "hard" selling or clever and driving arguments. People like to buy—not to be pushed into propositions, not to be "sold." However, you have to create this buying situation by interesting them in your proposition in the first place and then by listening to them. They will then sell themselves or provide you with clues to objections they have, which you can counter by showing that the benefits far outweigh the costs.

Always use questions like "How do you feel about that?"; "What do you think of it?"; "You feel that this is rather expensive. What do you think a reasonable price would be for it?"; "Then you feel this might prove useful to you if the price was ____ or if we could deliver it by ____ or if you could have it altered to suit?"

However, persuading someone of the advantage of a proposal is not the same as getting him to buy. When you have secured his approval of your proposition, always clinch the sale: "Good, can we get started next Monday?"; "Would next Thursday or Friday be convenient?"; "Would you like to sign the papers now?"; "Can we put down that Mr. Smith will present his report to the next meeting?"

YOURSELF

The motto of one of my schools was *res non verba*—roughly, "deeds not words" (*res* = things). This is a fine precept and it would be wonderful to think that our good work (or what would have been good work except for circumstances usually beyond our control or because of the mistakes of others) should be a sufficient justification and recommendation for ourselves in our working lives. To some extent, and in some occupations, this is so—or at least more true than in others—but not in management, where we are largely working by controlling and influencing other people. To them, we are a voice and an appearance—they see us and hear us. What we look like to them and what we say to them is quite literally "us."

You know that each of you appears differently to everyone with whom you come into contact. People are notoriously subjective about others, and they interpret in terms of their own emotional history the presentation or outward appearance of those they meet. For example, if you were bullied at school by a boy with red hair, then men with red hair will not look quite the same to you as they would, for example, to a lady whose first boyfriend had red hair. However, you are always left with yourself.

Work measurement teaches us that all work is broken down into tiny elements, many repetitive and common to many activities. Psychology teaches us that the same is true of our personal mannerisms and speech. We tend to accept ourselves as we are, but just as we should put ourselves into others' shoes (empathy) to understand, motivate, influence, and help them, we should catalog our own elements of behavior and compare them with standard practice (see Chapter 4).

How do you speak and look? What sort of people do you get along with best? Are they the sort of people you are, or were, or think you are, or would like to be? What are their characteristics? Does this analysis tell you anything about yourself?

When we are dealing with groups, we do best if somehow we seem part of the group and not as someone different, or as a stranger. The exception is if we are cast in some role—leader, chairman, consultant, doctor, or minister—where the group expects us to behave in a particular way. This applies to all encounters with others, and we are very much influenced by how people act, appear, and react the first time we meet them.

Meeting Other People

A meeting is always a test—for both people—and it will succeed best if you either seem familiar or have some neutral contact with the other people involved. For example, compare: "I was at school with your chairman" with "my daughter is in the same class as your daughter."

Comments about mutual acquaintances, places, hobbies, and interests, questions which give the other person a chance to talk about his or her main interest areas, all help. It is also good to be consistent.

People pigeonhole you, and if you behave and appear differently to them on different occasions, they will react inconsistently, too. How do you want to be pigeonholed? If it is as a manager, dress and act as your colleages would expect a manager to. Do you?

When talking prepare or think out what you have in mind beforehand. Do not be rushed into saying something you are not ready to say, or should not say. Many people will try to push you into saying more than you intend to, so work out a number of devices that will help you avoid answering without appearing discourteous in any way or without interrupting the flow of conversation (see Chapter 9).

More generally, be interested in what you are saying, without being childishly overenthusiastic. Appear confident and motivated. Look at your opposite numbers; gauge their reactions; pick up their smiles, shrugs, grimaces, and other body semantics; and show that you are with them and that you understand their feelings—even if you were the one who caused them to feel that way! If you talk too quickly, you may lose your listeners and you will fail to emphasize your subject, so talk quickly when you do not want maximum attention—that is, when you're talking about costs, disadvantages, or uninteresting details.

Pauses emphasize the phrases and words that immediately precede and follow them. Speak more slowly and pause to emphasize major benefits and points. Vary your pitch—your audience will soon learn that, for example, you talk a little louder when you need maximum attention from them. Never bore people: a monologue delivered in a monotone, with no humor or relief, does not endear you to anyone. (But be very careful about actual jokes. I suggest you never use them until you know your audience.)

Listen to your voice on a tape recorder or watch yourself on closed circuit television. See if you have any faults, and practice to correct them.

DEALING WITH SENIOR MANAGEMENT

One sometimes sees in job advertisements or descriptions the requirement that the person be able to negotiate "at top management level." In the industrial and commercial hierarchy it is sometimes said that "top" or "senior" management is a different breed of people, who behave in a different way from their junior colleagues.

But most top management people were promoted from junior management positions. Some grooming does take place, but the fact remains that senior management people are ordinary mortals who are where they are because of experience, special knowledge, ability, and sometimes luck. However, the exercise of power, influence, and leadership has an effect on people, and there are certain characteristics that they need to assume. Let us now explore these features.

A boss never loses his temper. A boss may occasionally be irritable and snappy, but must never be angry unless he is doing it deliberately to achieve some political effect.

You should not lose your temper or self-control with a boss. He may understand it, but he will not respect you. And since he will never really lose his cool, you will lose any status you may have had in the meeting.

Boardrooms are also "courts." People become successful partly because they want the respect and admiration of others. Always they are the target for opportunists, none more so than their colleagues who need their cooperation. At the board level, men are polite and courteous. They are always talking to each other, always making colleagues and subordinates feel important. You should act politely and (directly or indirectly) drop whatever compliments you can without being too obvious or fulsome. The compliment must be a clear one, although the better you know the person, the more positive and direct you can become. He will reciprocate and you should be agreeably modest and flattered—on the surface—but underneath you must always be thinking of the next point.

You may wish to disagree with your director or to criticize some aspect of his policy or actions. Of course you should only do so when it might serve some useful purpose: for example, if there is a disaster that was unavoidable or is unlikely to recur, it is better to avoid comment. Where there is some chance that your views will help the director make a better decision or use a better method of action, try to be tactful. For example: "With all due respect, sir, . . ."; or "You have obviously taken into account that the union will be opposed . . ."; or "I did mention, didn't I, that Mr. X said he was . . .?" Or even a hint would be enough: "You did say, sir, you would be seeing Mrs. Y first, didn't you?" or "Perhaps it's my fault, but I didn't quite understand the bit about. . . ."

Don't be too frightened of top executives; most of them are big boys and can take quite a few hard knocks. There is a law of nature which reduces resentment in proportion to the increase in difference in seniority. Equals and near-equals are much more sensitive than very senior and very junior people, although everyone is much too sensitive about themselves—never about your feelings!

Top executives are not always busy men. Good ones control their time; others may not have many departmental responsibilities, but they have a wide range of matters on their minds. Their attention span tends to be very limited, so if you have something to say, make sure you can say it quickly and succinctly.

"Something to say" is not sufficient. Senior managers are sometimes compared with big guns: they have to be pointed in the right direction and then fired. Directors understand that many decisions will have to be made by those below them, and they accept this role. However, if you point the gun in the wrong direction, then you will cease to have the director's trust, and because he cannot or will not spend the time with you, you are no longer able to get him to use his position on your behalf.

"Something to say" is something to remember and something to assimilate when the mind may be full of other things. Some top managers make lightning decisions, but most sit down and carefully work through anything important. Therefore, you will find that they often ask you to put it in writing. The ability to put a proposition in writing is a valuable skill, but it is not part of this chapter. However, if you have your proposition in writing before you say it to him, and, when asked to "put it in writing," you can hand over your piece of paper then and there, it will have much more impact and can even be of a lower literary standard!

What you propose to the director must be in such a form that he can assimilate it quickly—and can also use it. There are lots of pieces of interesting information with which you can burden his mind, but stick to specific proposals he can approve, promote, or act on. On his side, he may try to put you at your ease with questions about family, work, and so on, but do little more than answer his questions pleasantly and politely. Sometimes he may lead you into talking about matters still under negotiation elsewhere or into making comments on other people. Do not assume that he will respect your confidences, and do not assume that, if put in the position of talking to a powerful person of strong personality when you have not considered in advance what you might say, you may not find yourself saying something ill-considered or something that you wished you had not said.

Examples must relate more to an attitude of mind than to specific tactics to use, but compare the following:

CEO: How is your project getting on?

You: Fine, thanks. The report should be available in three weeks' time.

CEO: What are you going to propose?

You: Well, we haven't discussed it with the divisional manager yet.

CEO: But you can tell me. I won't hold you to anything at this stage.

You: _____ (How do you continue?)

You made your mistake in saying that the project was nearly finished. Could "Fine, thanks, we are just discussing the analyses with the divisional manager" have given him the right lead? But try continuing.

You: Certainly. We are scheduled for a meeting with the divisional manager next week. Much of our analysis covered the planning in the machine shop, as you know, and I think you know the problem areas we are dealing with. In fact, I was in the machine shop last week when the buyer from Company X was on his visit, and it occurred to me that. . . .

or

You: Certainly. We have been working on a number of alternative solutions to the problem, and I think that before long we can offer you something you will be interested to hear. We have a meeting with the divisional manager next week and should be able to present our findings to you shortly after that.

CEO: Come on, you are holding something back on me, you crafty so and so.

You: Well confidentially, sir, it would help a lot if you could give the divisional manager some credit for the results. Can I fix a meeting for next week? Are you likely to be in on Thursday or Friday?

or

You: We are not quite ready with the answers yet, but I will come and

see you or let your secretary know just as soon as we have anything ready for you to consider. In fact, I would appreciate the
opportunity of discussing this with you again before my presentation, since there are going to be some points on which I would
value your advice or help.

Directors are often involved in political struggles or games. Seldom
is there enough power and prestige for all to be satisfied. Big responsibilities mean big risks and big problems. If you put matters to them,
they may want or need to interpret and act on them in the light of these
struggles; they are also accustomed to taking the credit for work done
in their areas. It can be galling to see the project on which you have
slaved for months suddenly whisked out of your hands and treated as
the work of someone else—and with your name perhaps never even
being mentioned!

There can be cause for concern, but you may find that the great
man recognizes your work but is too busy or preoccupied to show it.
Senior managers require results, and they are accustomed to looking
for and recognizing the ability to produce those results. This ability is
best displayed by actually producing results.

Agreement by Attribution

There is one technique for gaining agreement which has to be used
sometimes—"agreement by attribution." This involves attributing an
idea or proposal to someone else—usually the one opposing it. It can
be carried out in stages:

Stage 1.
PROPOSER: Can we do X?
SENIOR MANAGER: No

Stage 2 (two weeks later, after heavy lunch with senior manager).
PROPOSER: Do you remember, you asked me to look into
X? Well, I am working on it and I think you
were probably quite correct and it will work.
SENIOR MANAGER: (*Confused grunt.*)

Stage 3 (two weeks later, under similar circumstances).
PROPOSER: I have finished the work on X and you were

> right after all (eyes shine slightly). I suppose I'd
> better get on and circulate the divisions this
> week?

SENIOR MANAGER: Yes.

This is not a set recipe for success, and the above sequence is a very crude one to make the point clearly, but it is amazing how often this type of approach can be introduced into negotiations. Just think for a moment why it would work. (And, of course, we are sure you will have thought of it yourself already. In fact, you mentioned it the last time we met!)

A common variant of this game is to attribute the proposal or the support for it to somebody powerful, such as the managing director or chairman. But you have to be very sure of your ground if you do this, and you will not be securing acceptance so much as acquiescence. (For example, "Shall I tell the CEO, then, that you don't want to go?" Answer: "OK, I'll go.")

Phrases to Avoid

The following phrases are best avoided:
   As a matter of fact
   So to speak
   You can believe me when I tell you
   It may or may not surprise you to know
   Between you and me
   Let's put it this way
   More or less
   Right
   In other words
   In any case
   "I"
   I think
   In my opinion
   According to my experience
   If I were in your place
   I can tell you
   Take my advice

Remember what I said
I must say this
I'm telling you

Also avoid:

Long speeches
Confrontations
Too much or too little enthusiasm
Formality
Unfavorable role expectations

Try to achieve:

Integration (shirt-sleeve approach)
Working meetings (all "we," and no "they")
Feedback: a response after not more than two hundred words (the response need not always be spoken)

Small Language Differences

Less good	Better
I think	Don't you think
I can tell you the answer to that	You can work out that answer yourself
You probably haven't thought of that	You're probably aware of
Your certificate must be attached	Please attach your certificate
You didn't conduct that interview very well	Did that interview go as well as you hoped?
Have you any comments to make?	How do you feel about that?
Do this immediately	Can we get started right away?

Selling Phrases

Less good	Better
You ought to stock a dozen of these; we're coming out with a big ad campaign.	You can make a nice profit from a dozen of these during our ad campaign.

We are buying twice as much this year. Can we have a price reduction?

Can we think about a bonus on our yearly turnover?

Suppose you were to die tomorrow—what would happen to your family?

Suppose you had died yesterday—what would have happened to your family?

How many gallons?

Shall I fill it up?

How many would you like?

Twenty or fifty?

Do you want a salad?

Would you care for a boiled egg—or a poached egg?

Do you want to buy a tie as well?

This tie matches your shirt.

Anything else? (Answer: "No.")

Is that all? (Answer: "Yes.")

When can we meet again to discuss this?

Would next Tuesday or Thursday afternoon be convenient for our next meeting?

Do you prefer coffee or tea?

Would you like to sign the order now?

You could sign the authorization now. Would you like to use my pen or yours?

Exercises

1. Consider when you last failed to persuade someone else of an important point. Analyze the reasons for your lack of success, and consider how you could have made your approach better. What factors would have had the most influence on his decision?
2. Which is the most effective in securing acceptance—quality or utility?
3. When did you last reject a proposal made to you? What were your stated reasons, and were they different from your real reasons?
4. When did you last accept a proposal made to you? What were your motives in accepting, and what did you like about the way the proposal was put? Would you have agreed anyway?
5. Are you having difficulties because you cannot persuade someone else to agree with you on a particular matter? (Everyone does!) Write down three possible reasons in the other person's mind for disagreeing with you, and consider what could be put forward to deal with or offset those objections.

PART
III

ADDITIONAL TECHNIQUES

Yet fish there be, that neither hook nor line,
Nor snare, nor net, nor engine can make thine:
They must be grop'd for, and be tickled too,
Or they will not be catched, whate'er you do.

JOHN BUNYAN

11 Recruitment: Selection and Induction

SELECTION

The purpose of recruitment is, normally, to find the right person for a particular job. The first steps must therefore be to define what the job is and what are the likely characteristics of the "right" person—that is, a job description and a candidate specification.

This discipline should always be undertaken. Not only does it make the subsequent selection processes easier and more efficient, but it enables the results of the selection (successes or failures on the job) to be reviewed against the original criteria to see if they need modification. It also helps to offset the personal bias—positive or negative—that every interviewer has with regard to particular personal or career characteristics.

Job Description

The main headings in a job description will include the following:

1. Job title.
2. Position in company—to whom the person is responsible, and details of subordinate positions (if any).
3. Main purpose of the job.
4. Key tasks to be carried out.
5. Any special limitations or rules.
6. Characteristics of subsequent work if the position is that of a trainee or is introductory in nature.
7. Location.
8. Conditions of employment.

Candidate Specification

The main headings in a candidate specification will include:

1. *Age range.*

2. *Education and qualifications.* A good educational history and good qualifications indicate a degree of excellence—intelligence, application, and ambition. Qualifications have not been given too much prominence at office level, but it must be remembered that with the expansion of further education, the proportion of bright people who did not go on to college has declined. It also means that the proportion of slow-witted people with further qualifications has increased, and that therefore the selection process has to be undertaken with greater care.

3. *Experience.* This should indicate at least the minimum experience necessary, and the ideal for the job.

4. *Personal characteristics.* What kind of people get on best with you and your staff? What kind get on best with the customers, and are there any qualities or characteristics that would help balance your team?

5. *Potential intentions.* One should consider the future requirements of the company—and, if applicable, the division or branch.

6. *Background* (mobility, family ties, being "local").

The first two steps can be considered as "rules," but the remainder of the selection process is a series of alternative strategies. The manager will have to choose for himself, depending on the situation and circumstances, but the subsequent notes offer some suggestions.

Advertising

The ideal classified ad states the company, the job, the location, and the salary. However, there are occasions when you have to weaken the impact of the advertisement by using box numbers and vague phrases like "salary according to experience." You should do this only where to be more specific might give away commercially useful information, where you are advertising the job of somebody who is to be replaced or transferred, and where the wages or conditions offered would give rise to jealousy on the part of the existing staff. Sometimes you will make a salary offer on the basis of the experience of the successful applicant, but then you may really be inviting two or more categories of people to apply—for example, intermediate counter clerk or senior counter clerk. In this case, you could specify two salary ranges or advertise two jobs.

Remember, staff is not attracted by vague advertisements. However, advertising costs money and, as stated above, can sometimes be embarrassing. You may have no alternative, but there are two methods you may want to consider:

1. You have a rough general idea of your staff turnover. Keep appropriate contact with the local employment service agency, professional and executive register, and so on. Make local contacts and interview likely people on a relaxed basis. Your present or past staff is a good source of contacts once it is known that you are ready to talk to interested people. When the vacancy finally occurs, you will then have a number of likely candidates to contact.

2. There are not enough experienced staff people, say, in the travel trade. Hence, there is salary competition and extensive raiding of other companies' staffs. If your budget can stand it, there is a lot to be said for taking on a bright beginner and bringing him along yourself. As soon as he moves into a more senior position, you can bring in another trainee.

Interviewing

Candidates remember interviews. When Company X is mentioned, it is quite common for someone to say, "Oh, yes, I was once interviewed by them for a job." Others may keep quiet for a variety of reasons, particularly if the interview was a failure. Candidates are not only potential employees of your company or your competitors; they are also potential or actual customers, and the effect on them of the interview may be significant. For the same reason, correspondence about applications, interviews, and results should be prompt and courteous—even if you are only going to indicate a delay.

As soon as I lose interest in a candidate for a job, I am as pleasant as I possibly can be, and try to give the subsequent impression that he or she only just missed a wonderful job with our wonderful firm. It would be unethical to give people too much in the way of false hopes, but it does no good to damage the generally pitifully limited self-confidence of most interviewees.

Interviews take time, and despite your care in preparing job descriptions and candidate specifications (and perhaps in applying the techniques described in Chapter 7), you are conscious that you are not a trained job interviewer and that it is a rather occasional exercise as far as you are concerned.

If you can, get applicants to write a letter with personal details, and then get them to fill in an application form. The form ensures that all the personal details are provided for in a standard—and therefore easily compared—manner, but it serves another purpose as well: few applicants keep copies of their original letters, and if they have been "improving" their qualifications, you may find discrepancies between the information in the letter and on the form.

It will help if you can send or give the applicant a copy of the job description and any company leaflet or write-up to read before the interview. Likewise you should read his particulars again before he comes in, and in that way the interview will be free of unnecessary discussion. The bulk of the interview should be devoted to an assessment of how well he will perform in the job and in the department.

Interview Strategy

The next thing to do is to formulate your interview strategy. You should decide whether to have one or two interviews. In fact, there is a company which has decided that interviewing is such a faulty process that it selects its appointees on the basis of their applications. I do not suggest that you do this, but you should consider whether a single interview will suffice. Interviewees perform differently on different occasions, and so do interviewers, and you may want to see the person twice, or you may want somebody else in your office or from another branch or head office to give a second opinion if the results of a wrong choice would be particularly disastrous.

Having decided who is to do the interviewing and how many interviews there are to be, and having done your preparation for them, then the question arises as to how to conduct the interview. Normally interviews are conducted behind the desk; however, if you want to be less formal and to get the person being interviewed to be as close and as cooperative as possible, then it is better either to sit beside him or to sit opposite him in a low chair to create as "non-office-like" a situation as possible. You may, in fact, decide that you do not want an informal interview. Some people advocate that a "stress" interview is better, because the work situation that the person will have to encounter may well be one in which he or she is under considerable stress.

A framework or method for the interview should be set up. Where a choice has to be made (and justified) between several candidates, similar questions or tests should be applied. The results and the interviewers' impressions should be noted at the time to provide comparative information for the final selection. Obviously, you are comparing each candidate against the job description and candidate specification, and annotated copies of these can be used as an *aide-mémoire* in the interview. These other kinds of tests should be considered:

Skill tests
Specific knowledge
Reaction to situations
Intelligence and temperament

Skill tests. These are tests designed to see how well particular operations can be performed. Examples are asking a typist to type a document or a clerk to compose a reply to a letter.

Specific knowledge. This would be for people with some experience, and would involve asking questions about the procedures, products, and services relevant to the company, trade, or job. Experience and knowledge are related, but there is a difference between the person who can answer, "Yes, I know how to do that—you start by . . ." and the person who can answer, "Yes, I know how to do that and I have done it many times. You start by. . . ."

Reaction to situations. This is a very valuable test, and it offers some of the most reliable pointers to future performance. You describe a situation—perhaps a customer complaint, a refund situation, a cancellation by a supplier or principal, an argument with a colleague—and ask them how they would handle it and what their attitude might be.

Intelligence and temperament. These are scientific tests of different kinds which measure various abilities and aptitudes and ascertain the weighting of various personality characteristics. As a general rule, tests of this kind should be applied with expert help, but they can provide a specific measure of comparison and a clear indication of ability. At good bookstores it is possible to buy simple intelligence tests that are quite reliable, as a measure of mental potential, and to apply them yourself, using the directions.

Sometimes, people will be coming to you from a different type of occupation, and a fair test in these cases is to ask them to display their ability in their present job. For example, if the person has been an assistant in a shoe store, it might be reasonable to ask her to sell you a pair of shoes, or if the person has been in an accounts department, it might be an idea to ask her to explain to you the accounts procedure or part of it. Although it may be difficult to ask people to display ability in subjects they know nothing about, it is, I think, reasonable to feel that if an applicant cannot perform well in his present job, then you should consider very seriously whether he will perform well in a new job.

Interview Length

You have decided your interview strategy, and you must also decide the interview length. In some cases the interview may run on, but generally the more menial the job, or the more limited the person being interviewed, the shorter the interview will be. For example, a cleaner's job or a clerk-typist's job may require an interview of 10–20 minutes perhaps, or two interviews of 10 or 20 minutes each, if you are going to conduct two interviews, whereas to interview someone for the position of, say, chairman of your company might require a number of interviews of several hours' duration—not that we are envisaging your being involved in that at the moment!

The Choice

Let us move on for a little while and consider some other matters that affect the process of interviewing and selection. There is the question of what to do if two suitable people turn up, or if none turn up who are suitable, or if the person who is best as a result of interviews is mediocre (in other words, he or she would "do," but you are not terribly happy about it). Common sense dictates the answers to these questions, with the exception, perhaps, of the last one.

If an excessively good clerk joins your branch, that may present problems (although they may be problems that you will probably be happy to have). If you make a real mistake in selection, the answer to that situation is also very plain. There is, however, a much bigger difficulty in disposing of people who perform reasonably well but not well enough to give you full satisfaction. If one is looking for a rule in a situation like this, the answer is to keep the mediocre person on the hook and keep on trying to find somebody in whom you have more confidence.

In an interview you are very dependent on what candidates tell you. They should, however, have done some preparation, particularly if you have provided them in advance with the job description and with company details. It is a good idea to ask them whether they know anything about your company. It is a sign of initiative at least if they have taken the trouble to find out something about the work or your office before they come, or at least have read what has been sent to them.

I knew a chairman who used to ask applicants whether they thought they could do the job—in other words, he shared the decision with the candidate. However, most candidates will press on with an interview whether or not they think they are suitable or interested, simply because they do not like to be rejected. It is quite a boost for the candidate to be offered a job, even if he knows he is going to turn it down: he does not like to think he did not have the chance of turning it down because he was not selected.

One problem that faces the manager is that he may occasionally find somebody who is really suitable—someone in whom he is fully confident and whom he really wants. In such circumstances, there may be some merit in offering the job straightaway at the interview in order to prevent the candidate from going to other interviews, or at least to discourage him from doing so. If a commitment can be obtained then and there, you may have forestalled a situation in which when the person receives the offer two or three days later, he will have already been somewhere else and received another offer.

References

As I said, you are very dependent on how the person performs during an interview, and this is where references come in. Your company policy may be to have the man checked medically, and to accept written references from previous employers. You may wish to do this anyway, but remember that written references are becoming progressively less useful as a means of identifying people who have some disadvantages, or who have perhaps been unsatisfactory in their previous job. (For example, would you give a bad reference to somebody whom you wanted to get rid of?)

There are also a large number of ways in which written references or references obtained from companies can be falsified. This chapter would be wrong to describe these in writing, but there are many ways in which the employee with a bad history can cover up spells in prison, defalcations, poor recommendations, and the like. The least unreliable way of obtaining a reference is to actually telephone the candidate's current manager after the decision to offer the job has been made, and then to see if, by the way he answers, you can get some reliable information.

You will, of course, be familiar with the technique of asking the same questions more than once at different times in the interview, and note if there is any difference in the person's answers. You can also ask questions obliquely so that the answer to what you really want to know is given when the person is off guard. You may also want to ask him questions about things previously discussed to see if he has been concentrating and has learned a point that was made in the exchange.

When the Candidate Is Uncertain

Now, just as you are very dependent on the interviewee's performance at the interview, so he is very dependent on your performance for getting an idea of the job he is to take. In certain cases, the candidate will not be certain that the job which you are offering is the one for him or not. This may work two ways; he may take a chance and subsequently find that he wants to leave you; or he may be discouraged and turn the job down, whereas in fact he would have been successful and happy with you. If it is at all possible, let him meet the other staff (perhaps over a cup of coffee), see where he would be working, and get some idea of the work involved. Career counselors at several schools are now advising young people to do this before taking a job.

ORIENTATION

We have considered ways of improving our selection and interviewing, but we can never be completely certain of success. We take a snapshot of the applicant and decide on his or her suitability, but the situation is a dynamic one. We have all had the experience where an appointment goes sour on us, and this is not always a mistake in selection, although it may appear to be one. Many promising recruits are "ruined" within a few weeks of joining a company, and this section of the chapter sets out some methods of avoiding this.

Basic Points

Do you remember your first day at school, your first day at work, your first day in your present job? They were days of mixed expectations, hopes, and emotions; days when impressions and incidents bit deep and went a long way to forming your attitudes to what you had started. Those impressions were important to you, and therefore important to your company—and in particular, when you were young, impressionable, and mobile.

Companies go to great lengths to attract and employ the "right" people, but despite the effort and expense, many employees leave after a short period or turn out not to be so "right" when they are in the post. Of course, mistakes will be made in selection—there are staff for whom the company or work turns out to be not what they thought it would be, or what they wanted, and vice versa—but our experience is that a significant proportion are put off by unsatisfactory happenings in their first days on the job. Their orientation procedure has not been planned or implemented in the best way.

Orientation also refers to promotions and transfers, and it is most important to ensure that those newly appointed to supervisory positions are given guidance in the practice of managing others so that they get off to the most advantageous start. In this chapter, we are concentrating on the first day of the new entrant—a day that may help mold a person's attitudes to work and to his employer for the rest of his life.

Needs of the Company and the Individual

What does the company want of the new entrant? The company wants the person:

To be doing a useful job quickly
To stay and be assimilated
To develop as quickly as possible

On the other hand, the individual wants:

To respect his employer
To understand the purpose of his job and work
To be useful
To be recognized as a person
To see recognition of skills and attainments, if he has any
To feel "at home" (social, psychological aspects)
To enjoy his working life
To see where it is all leading (next task, career, money prospects)

I would suggest that these needs are very close to each other, unless you take the view that the person just wants to give as little as possible and take as much as he can, or is basically uninterested in anything called discipline, respect, learning, work, and so on. However, you should consider what to do if he is. Would you act differently in his place?

The important thing is to get him doing a useful and sensible task at the earliest opportunity. Train him for the next task and always give him a little more than you are sure he can handle. Train, stretch, congratulate him; make him feel he is moving as far as he can go. Do not bore good youngsters by keeping them on routine or "junior" jobs too long.

Day of Arrival

See the new entrant when he arrives, and give him a 10–20 minute chat before you settle him down to his first task. That initial introduction is a source of tension for both sides, and should be prepared and adjusted to the circumstances. We suggest that you not overwhelm him with all the background information at once. Remember that he is just as concerned with minor administration matters (for example, where to put his coat; the position of toilets; lunch or coffee-break procedures), but he doesn't need to find out everything in the first day or two. However, he should be told the following:

1. The general scale and organization of the company.
2. What types of business are transacted.
3. Any special features about the branch.
4. The purpose of what he does and why he was recruited.
5. What he will do next. (These are questions which his relatives and friends will ask him on his return.)
6. Your position or authority. Local and company rules and etiquette. (You are the company to him. If you are cheerful, enthusiastic, competent, what will he think? On the other hand, if you are cynical, hardbitten, overly busy, quick-tempered, what will be think then?)

Answer his questions, but do not spend too long chatting. He came to work and wants to be useful. Get him doing something useful. Get him doing something useful and relevant without delay. Only one rule: do not overdo it during orientation, but do spend time with him at the beginning, and do not ignore him for any long period—you are very important to him.

Some organizations have printed orientation booklets, but it can be a good idea to give him a little outline plan of the office with colleagues' names, your own name and title, telephone number, and other important points he might easily forget to his embarrassment in the first day or so.

Come back to him at intervals. Encourage him, give him more tasks, more training. Do not let him get away with anything sloppy, but be patient until he has gotten the message.

Orientation Checklist

The following checklist summarizes the main points to bear in mind, although of course each individual will need to be treated on his or her own merits. However, if you are too busy to see your new staff member when he joins, just consider what will be going on in his mind.

Give the new entrant the following information:

1. Who and what you are. How he should address you.
2. The job, section, and branch titles.
3. Check his experience and skill, if any, and find out any proclivities he may have.
4. Work times, coffee breaks, lunch, cloakroom arrangements, his desk, stationery, how and when his paycheck arrives, and any other office rules.
5. The company—that is, its business and the business of the branch or the department.
6. His colleagues—introduce them and hand out or construct with him a list of their names and functions and any points of style which may help him.
7. Answer any questions.

People learn fastest and work best for supervisors they respect and like. Does your orientation procedure, appearance, and style command respect, or does it need to be more helpful, polite, efficient, enthusiastic, disciplined, and so on? Perhaps if he is not learning, then you are not teaching him the right way. Remember that "there are no bad staff people, only bad supervisors and managers."

Exercises

1. Prepare a job description for your own job, and have it discussed and approved by your superiors.
2. Prepare a job specification for your job and compare it with your own particulars.
3. Prepare job descriptions for your subordinates, and in particular your deputy—whether you have one or not.
4. Prepare a ten-minute orientation talk (about 1,500 words, but it could be done in headings) and use it when the next recruit arrives in your department.

A soft answer turneth away wrath, but grievous words stir up anger. PROVERBS 15:1

12 Appraisal and Counseling

APPRAISAL

We are appraising each other, consciously and subconsciously, most of the time. Our subordinates judge us, and we judge them. Everybody is forming views or confirming previous impressions of others all the time. It gives us a natural satisfaction to understand how people react and feel.

Likewise, we are happy to advise or counsel others whenever they ask us to or when we feel the conditions are right, provided always that the situation is one in which our advice or comments are not going to cause resentment. We like to help others, and to a considerable extent helping others is one of the primary objectives of appraisal and counseling.

Appraisal and counseling become "subjects" because in the pressure of normal business we may not spend enough time or give sufficient consideration to them. We have to make sure they are done in a structural fashion and that we prepare ourselves to give proper attention to all the necessary aspects. Information has to be sought and given. Proper communication must be established if appraisal and counseling are to succeed.

Matters to Be Established

Various matters need to be established, although not necessarily all at the same time. These will include:

Review of performance and achievements
Points of weakness and warnings
Training and development needs
Fitness in work and job satisfaction
Prospects and career development
Review of job description and requirements
Salary review
Manpower planning assessments ("tiering")
Personal matters

You may not have the answers for everything, and there is a limit to waving the magic wand in any situation. However, the interviewee expects positive suggestions, actions, and follow-up, and the good manager prepares in advance by thinking of what could and might be done.

Criticism

Criticism, we said, raises defensive issues, leads to arguments, and has a negative effect on subsequent performance. However, we cannot avoid some criticism, even if it is done by implication, and there are occasions when the errors are of such a significance that they have to be dealt with explicitly and formally. This is a problem, and the reason is simply that the other person feels he is being attacked. The fact that the attack is psychological, not physical, makes it no less real, although more difficult to control.

Praise

We put forward a case for participation and objectivity, but there are two other methods to consider. One is praise. Every employee will have done, or will have intended to do, something useful (otherwise he should not be on your staff!), and this should be recognized at the outset of any review session. Salesmen call this the "sandwich technique," starting and finishing a discussion with something that is attractive or that appeals to the other's ego. Praise or recognition must be part of the review, but it can be used to balance the bad news. "You have made a good start on such and such, and now you can really begin to tie things together by. . . ."

Constructive Suggestions

The other point is to put forward constructive suggestions. Criticism is discouraging, but positive proposals for new standards, goals, or objectives (or for training, advice, or help) have an encouraging effect. This is particularly true where the employee has suggested the proposals or has contributed to them. There must be a clear method or means of obtaining the required improvement: the employee must feel he knows (and approves of) what is required, and how he can produce it. These points will be considered in more detail, but they represent a formidable list.

Appraisal Sessions

Many managers view a cold-blooded appraisal session with apprehension—and rightly so. Such interviews are very sensitive and personal and can easily lead to misunderstandings. They invite proposals for action on either side, which may in themselves create problems or be difficult to follow up.

Criticism may result in the elimination of faults ("All right, you want it that way, you'll get it that way"), but it has a negative effect on subsequent motivation. However well-intentioned, it leads to a defensive attitude on the part of the person being assessed, and even if he recognizes the fault, he may feel that your method of presenting it is unfair.

Conducting appraisals in the form of discussion about performance is often the best way to give people information about themselves. Talk about actual results, comparing these with target figures, and ask the person for his reaction to what you have presented. Try not to wave "red flags" in front of people—emotionally charged phrases and statements that are likely to trigger defensive reactions. Instead, encourage the person to participate in his own evaluation. Ask him, "How do you feel about the situation?" or "Is . . . going as well as you'd hoped it would?" Even a simple "Is there anything I can do to help?" may encourage the interviewee to discuss his personal shortcomings with you. If a man criticizes himself, he feels he is participating, and is directing attention to areas which he wants to discuss. He feels that the interview is fair and objective.

To sum up, there are four keynotes to strike in the successful review:

1. Praise for achievement and intentions.
2. Participation at all points.
3. Objective approach to problems.
4. Means of obtaining specific improvements.

We have looked at the climate of and approach to the assessment. Depending on its policies, each company will be using the assessment procedure for slightly different purposes, and obviously whoever is doing the assessments must know what those purposes are. For completeness and standardization, assessments are written on a form; your company may have one already. Examples are given in Figures 12-1, 12-2, and 12-3.

Most of assessment is common sense, but we list now the steps involved in the concept, or in preparation.

The Six Principles

1. *What are we trying to appraise?* Competence in job and value to company.

2. *What criteria or qualities would be used to judge competence?* Go for critieria which are concrete and measurable. Go for the ones which really give a measure of performance: output and quality, as well as job knowledge, product knowledge, customer relations, cooperation, initiative, discipline, and bearing. Let us decide how many criteria we will use, and rank them in order of importance.

3. *What framework will we use?* Refer to the specimen forms. Consider what descriptions would be best—unsatisfactory, satisfactory, very good, outstanding, unproved. Or evaluate them along these lines: does not meet requirements, needs some improvement, meets job re-

---

STRICTLY PRIVATE AND CONFIDENTIAL

STAFF PERFORMANCE REPORT

SURNAME .... FIRST NAME(S) ....

Date of birth ....

DEPARTMENT .... JOB TITLE .... GRADE ....

Length of Service in .... Length of time in present job ....

Date of Previous Review ....

PART 1   To be completed by Job Holder

    i. Have there been any special office or domestic circumstances that have affected your performance of the job during the period under review?

    Please answer Yes or No .... If "Yes", what were they?

    ii. Are there ways in which the Company can help you do your job better?

    iii. Would you like the opportunity to change your job within the Company?

    Please answer Yes or No ....

    If "Yes", please explain what jobs you would prefer and why? Are there any abilities which you possess that you feel can be useful to the Company in other work? For example, previous business experience, further education or personal aptitudes.

Date ....   Signed ....

Figure 12-1. Specimen staff performance report.

quirements, exceeds requirements, far exceeds requirements. Five is the normal range of rankings.

4. *How often will we appraise?* Consider salary and cost-of-living reviews. Every six months is considered good practice for formal appraisals.

PART 2   To be completed by the Job Holder's immediate superior

From the assessment on the Merit Rating form PART 3 and your
knowledge of the staff member please indicate:

   i. What are the member of staff's strong points?

   ii. What points need improving?

   iii. How are you helping the Job Holder to improve on these points?

   iv. How do you intend to develop this member of staff during the next
     review period?

   v. Overall Assessment from PART 3.

   vi. Previous overall assessment.

   vii. General comments which should include any aspects of the Job Holder's
      qualities or performance that are not covered above.

Figure 12-1. Part 2.

5. *Who should do it?* The manager should know the person best.
Therefore, he can assess performance comprehensively and objec-
tively. He can identify and offer assistance where performance is below
par, and give praise and recognition where it is above par. Is anyone
else involved? Who, if anyone, should receive copies of the assessments? Should there be second opinions or appeals? Apart from the
manager and the employee, can anyone take action to help?

6. *How much should staff be told?* Should the interviewee see all or
part of the final assessment, and should the form be completed in conjunction with him? On one hand, the employee wants to know how he

PART 3. MERIT RATING ASSESSMENT.			SURNAME AND INITIALS		DATE ....
FACTOR	DOES NOT YET MEET REQUIREMENTS (1)	NEEDS SOME IMPROVEMENTS (2)	MEETS JOB REQUIREMENTS (3)	EXCEEDS JOB REQUIREMENTS (4)	FAR EXCEEDS JOB REQUIREMENTS (5)
A. *Output* (Compared with standard)	Slow	Reasonable but not yet up to standard.	Satisfactory. Output to standard.	Works hard. Gets through more work than most.	Exceptionally quick and industrious worker.
B. *Quality/accuracy* (Compared with standard)	Inclined to make mistakes. Needs checking/close supervision.	Makes only few mistakes. Work reasonable.	Reliable and accurate. Very few mistakes. Satisfactory.	Good worker. Completely reliable and accurate.	Unusually good.
C. *Job knowledge*	New to the work. Needs help or direction to cope with the normal aspects of work.	Copes with all the regular aspects of the work with only routine supervision.	Able to perform the work virtually in all aspects. Occasional direction needed.	Complete knowledge of work. Can impart knowledge to others. Better than most.	Outstandingly capable, sound and complete knowledge of work. Very experienced.
D. *Co-operation*	Cooperates reluctantly.	Cooperative. Reasonably receptive to instructions.	Cooperative and accepts instructions willingly.	Very cooperative and flexible.	Exceptionally helpful.
E. *Initiative*	Shows no initiative.	Sometimes misses opportunities to show initiative.	Shows initiative required of the job.	Has particularly sound and practical ideas.	Extreme flexible and quick. An example to the department.
F. *Discipline/bearing*	Not a good timekeeper. Inclined to waste time. Presentation needs to be improved. Requires warning.	Satisfactory.	Good. Conscientious employee.	A good example and very conscientious.	Extremely conscientious in every way. Bearing and conduct exemplary.

Overall assessment: Taking all factors into consideration, check the phrase which most accurately describes the employee relative to your standard of a satisfactory performance of the work, and complete PART 2 Q. V.

1. *DOES NOT YET MEET REQUIREMENTS.*
   Only acceptable for a starter, below standard and must improve to be retained in existing job. ....

2. *NEEDS SOME IMPROVEMENT.*
   Regarded as adequate.

3. *MEETS JOB REQUIREMENTS.*
   A good employee. ....

4. *EXCEEDS JOB REQUIREMENTS.*
   A very good employee, ready to be considered for promotion. ....

5. *FAR EXCEEDS JOB REQUIREMENTS.*
   A very good employee in all respects
   (a) Does not seek promotion
   or (b) Promotion is overdue. ....

Figure 12-1. Part 3.

FACTOR	BELOW STANDARD (1)	ROOM FOR IMPROVEMENT (2)	EXPERIENCED (3)	ABOVE AVERAGE (4)	SUPERIOR (5)
1. *Job knowledge* How is he/she coping with the work? Has he/she learnt the work. Is help needed?	New to the work. Needing help or direction to cope with the normal aspects of work.	Coping with all the regular aspects of the work with only routine supervision.	Able to perform the work virtually in all aspects. Occasional direction needed.	Complete knowledge of work. Can impart knowledge to others. Better than most.	Outstandingly capable. Sound and complete knowledge of work. Very experienced.
2. *Productivity* Output of work compared with standard (not quality or accuracy).	Slow.	Reasonable but not satisfactory.	Satisfactory. Output to standard.	Works hard. Gets through more work than most.	Exceptionally quick and industrious worker.
3. *Quality* Is the work performed in a reliable and accurate manner?	Inclined to forget and make mistakes. Needs checking/close supervision.	Makes only few mistakes. Work reasonable.	Reliable and accurate. Very few mistakes. Satisfactory.	Good worker. Completely reliable and accurate.	Unusually good.
4. *Cooperation/initiative* Is he/she cooperative, willing to help others, to organize his/her work?	Cooperates reluctantly. Can be a source of friction.	Cooperative. reasonably receptive to instructions.	Cooperative and accepts instructions willingly. Organizes work well. Fits in well and is flexible.	Very cooperative and has sound and practical ideas. Sensible and flexible.	Exceptionally helpful and constructive, flexible and quick. An example to the department.
5. *Discipline/bearing* Does he/she start work promptly and continue until time to stop? Is his/her presentation reasonable?	Not a good timekeeper. Inclined to waste time. Presentation needs to be improved. Often requires warning.	Satisfactory.	Good. Conscientious employee.	A good example and very conscientious.	Extremely conscientious in every way. Bearing and conduct exemplary.

Overall assessment: Taking all factors into consideration, tick the phrase which most accurately describes the employee relative to your standard of a satisfactory performance of the work.

1. Only acceptable for a starter, below standard and must improve to be retained. ....
2. Regarded as adequate. ....
3. A good employee.

4. A very good employee, ready to be considered for promotion. ....
5. A very good employee is all respects, but doesn't seek promotion, or promotion is overdue. ....

Figure 12-2. Merit rating guide.

<table>
<tr><td colspan="2">Part One. In this part you should appraise the employee's strengths and weaknesses as shown by performance during the year. Mark each separate quality out of six (marks will not be totalled).</td></tr>
</table>

Excellent	6	Some problems	3
Very Good	5	Not satisfactory	2
Average	4	Untrained or untried	1

A) Performance in work	Marks
Knowledge and experience Application Adaptability Accuracy Supervisory ability General assessment	
B) Mental ability	
C) Relations with others	
D) Maturity and judgment	

Part Two. In this part you should make specific comments under the following headings:

Job successes and job failures

Particular strengths and weaknesses

Training and courses attended during part year — planned further training

Development potential, future plans for promotion or transfer

Morale and attitude to work and company

Additional remarks, including employee's points at assessment interview

NAME................................... DATE............... ASSESSOR.....................

Figure 12-3. Specimen assessment form.

is regarded, but on the other, the assessor or manager may find it embarrassing to be completely frank and to show critical comments in writing. Some companies have a two-part assessment, in which the employee sees and signs one part, but there is a confidential section which is not seen. This chapter does not offer an answer to this question; the management style of the company may provide an answer, but it is axiomatic that nothing should be done that does not strengthen the relationship between the management and employees or which damages any person's self-confidence. If you cannot be frank with your employees, what does that tell you about your own management style? Will the staff think that you are being honest with them?

COUNSELING

Part of an assessment review is advice and the determination of action to obtain improvements—that is, counseling is involved. However, there are specific counseling interviews, initiated by the member of the staff or by his manager, to deal with particular problems, often those of a personal nature.

The manager may be in a good position to help with private problems, and it may be appropriate for him to do so, either in his managerial capacity or just as any human being will try to help another. He is, however, employed primarily to keep the business going: he is a manager, not a psychiatrist.

Each manager must use his own judgment, but he should be careful about getting involved in difficult personal problems which he may not be able to handle. In such cases, the company personnel manager should be contacted, and if this is not feasible there are many agencies and organizations that can help (for example, social services departments, family planning associations, marriage guidance councils, citizens advice bureaus, the Samaritans), as well as your, or the employee's, lawyer, doctor, bank manager, or minister.

People should always feel that they can approach you, and that you "care," even if you do not provide all the answers yourself personally.

Exercises

1. Decide whether you want or need to install a formal appraisal and counseling system.
2. Consider whether there is any policy or experience in appraisals elsewhere in the organization that you should consult and whether you should develop a system in cooperation with them or on your own.
3. Define your attitude to the six principles discussed in this chapter.
4. Design your own appraisal form or checklist.

If the worker hasn't learned, then the trainer hasn't taught.

13 Teaching and Learning

Most managers can and do train subordinates and colleagues, and the world is full of people struggling to remember what to do, or trying to put mistakes right. This chapter sets out a method for training quickly and effectively, and it may help you save time (both your own and that of your staff) when you next become involved in the process.

METHOD

Concentration is difficult, so avoid anything that causes distractions or tensions. Has the trainee made himself comfortable and have you left instructions about phone calls and interruptions? Put him at ease: instruction is better at his desk or work position or in neutral surroundings. It is better to sit beside him than to talk with a desk between you.

Now start by telling him exactly what you are trying to do. For example: "I would like us to spend half an hour this afternoon checking through the requisitioning procedure," or "Would you like us to start looking at the XYZ machine so that you can begin to learn how to use it?" Then, find out what he knows or thinks he knows about it already. He may have had some experience or discussion on the subject elsewhere, which may be relevant to this situation.

Next, if you haven't already mentioned why he should learn what you are teaching, tell him: "This is the way we obtain the stationery, pencils, erasers, or similar things that we use in the office. I would like you to learn this, so that you can take it over from Mary." Or you can say, "we use this machine to cut the threads on the special bolts which support the girders in the crane assembly," or "it is worth getting to know how to use this procedure so that when Joe and I are away, you will be able to deal with any service requests." Get his interest. Make sure he sees some point in learning the job, and show your own appreciation of the importance of the task.

DEMONSTRATION

At this point you can explain the job or procedure. If any forms or equipment are involved, have them there to show wherever possible, and explain any technical terms, jargon, or abbreviations. Demonstration ("show-how") is invaluable, and, if you can, run over the job quietly at this stage so that the trainee can learn by watching and can get an overall view of the procedure.

Now think how much you are likely to be able to teach him on this occasion. People whose minds have not been trained cannot generally concentrate for more than about ten minutes on a lecture. Break up what you say to them into natural units, preferably 150–200 words, or one to two minutes, depending on how fast you talk, and let them react or catch up. For example, ask them, "Are you with me so far?" They can concentrate on "doing" rather than listening, but it is far better to teach a little but thoroughly, rather than confuse a person by covering too much ground.

Professional staff or graduates can concentrate for longer periods—say, up to 40 minutes—though it may be more difficult to hold their interest. Older people find it harder to learn new subjects, although they will often appear to follow what you say when they do not want to seem stupid.

So demonstrate the job again, in key stages one at a time, and ex-

plain fully in detail each stage as you go. Answer questions with toler-
ance and patience—everyone has a blank period from time to time. Do
not go on beyond the point at which confusion sets in. "Well, that's
about far enough for just now," you can say. "Let's have a recap, and
then you can try it out."

TRYING OUT

Next, get him to try out what you have just taught him,
in stages, and with you watching. Do not let him run ahead, because it
is just as easy to do the wrong thing as the right thing, and then the
wrong thing has to be unlearned before he can get it right. Do not let
him just run though it, because he may do the right things by mistake.

Point out any errors as they arise. Be helpful, not critical: if he
makes a real mess, ask him for his own opinion. "How do you feel
about that particular result?" "How do you think that went?" "What
happened that time?" "What went wrong?" Try not to damage his
confidence. "Well done," you can say. "You are getting the idea, but it
still isn't quite there. Let's have another try, and this time concentrate
more on getting the discount calculations exact!"

QUESTIONS

In due course ask him questions about the job and each
stage of it to make sure he really understands what he is doing. Use
your critical analysis questions, such as: How do you do that? Why is
that done? Where is that done? Where does that go? When does that
happen? What does that achieve? Who does that part of it? Which departments are involved?

Carry on until you are sure he knows the job and, of course, that he
has the necessary confidence that comes from proper training.

At that point he can start on his own, but never throw him off the
deep end, just like that. Make sure he knows to whom to turn if he
forgets something or if an unexpected situation arises. Do not ignore
him; show that you are still interested in the job and in his performance by checking with him—often at first, less often as he becomes
proficient. See if he has any questions and comments. People often like
to make a comment to share their experiences: "It makes your hands

tingle, doesn't it?" "Hot work today," "I don't know how I got away with that one," and so on.

Please ask one question if you have not already done so. Would not a manager who instructs like this get on the nerves of his staff? Phrases like "insulting my intelligence" or "fuss budget" come to mind. "Treat us like adults," they cry, and then proceed to get it wrong. The steps in this chapter can be very helpful, but only if you have a good working understanding with your subordinates.

By now, the trainee should have settled down to the job under normal supervision. You have done a solid piece of training, and you can tick off another task achieved on your training plan. You can trust him, and he feels you should. But alas, managers are not paid to ignore their staff. You must continue to show interest, and you must from time to time sit down with him and see what he is actually doing. Is it in accordance with the procedure? Is it right? You can only do this without offense or unease if you have that same relationship with your staff that comes through regular contact. What is regular contact? I leave that to you, but once a day used to be my rule. You also get that vital ingredient in control and communications—feedback.

Exercises

1. When did you last learn a major new task or procedure?
2. Were you taught or did you teach yourself? Did you learn it satisfactorily, or could it have been handled better?
3. Are internal memos or instructions sufficient for most staff to absorb changes?
4. How should training manuals be set out?
5. Have you got a training plan? (See Chapter 6.)
6. How are your people trained? Should you be involved more or less? If they are trained by others, are you satisfied with their training technique?
7. Are there any courses that would help? How could you justify them?
8. What is the difference in cost to the organization of a person's being taught on a two-week course and starting the job as 80 percent proficient, and the same clerk taking ten weeks to become 80 percent proficient (assuming a straight learning curve from zero to 80 percent during the period) by learning "on the job"?
    Cost of course: $480
    Cost of person: $200 per week.
    Answer: "value" in first case.

8 weeks × 80% of $200 = $1,280 − $480 (Cost of course) = $800.
In the second case:
10 weeks × 40% of $200 = $800.

9. Would you rather have properly trained people in your department, or have them milling around trying to pick up the job and perhaps making expensive mistakes?

10. Is the value of the people on staff determined by their wages, or is there another value?

A practical man is a man who practices the errors of his forefathers.
                                                    BENJAMIN DISRAELI

14   The Assessment and Improvement of Work

INTRODUCTION

In chapter 2 a method was put forward for using diary sheets and work distribution charts to enable the manager to get an overall view of how he was spending his own time, before starting a constructive analysis of his activities. The same approach can be applied to the work in your department as a whole, and this chapter indicates how it can be done. The result will be that you will finish up with information about how long each of the activities in your area takes, or, alternatively, you will finish up with an estimated work content for each transaction.

The value of this kind of information in costing and planning and in the improvement of procedures need hardly be pointed out. Subsequent chapters will explain in more detail how these can be progressed from the basic information obtained through the method. (Of course, if you already have detailed measurement in your area, then you shouldn't need to read this chapter.)

To examine the work in your department in proper perspective, you'll need a picture of the area as a whole plus individual breakdowns of the work of each individual.

ACTIVITY LIST

The activity list should be prepared by yourself, and should include all of the major activities that are performed, or that should be performed, to fulfill the objectives of the department. If, for example, a personnel manager felt that wage and salary surveys were an activity that his department should be performing but was not doing so at present, it should go on the list. This would show, of course, that you were aware of a need but were unable to devote any time at present for it. The heading "miscellaneous" is usually required for the odd jobs that do not contribute directly to the real purpose of the department. An example of the heading of an activity list is shown in Figure 14-1.

TASK LIST

The task list is a detailed record of each separate item of work performed by the individual. Each employee—including, of course, yourself—prepares his own list to ensure a clear coherent story, and you will later review these lists with your subordinates. Obviously the lists must be as complete as possible and the wording should be specific and not ambiguous. (By ambiguous, I mean expressions such as "checking" and "administration.") The type of entries that should appear on the task list might be, for example, "checking arrival of incoming shipments," "checking invoices against purchase orders and goods received notes," "replenishing stationery cupboards," "drawing stores," and so on. An example of the heading of a task list is shown in Figure 14-2.

TIME TAKEN FOR EACH ACTIVITY

You will see in the task list that provision is put in for the time taken for each activity. A common-sense answer in terms of representative times or estimates may be produced from estimates or records, but more often it is obtained by asking the person or persons concerned to keep a simple record for a few days.

DEPARTMENT:	SECTION:	SUPERVISOR:	DATE:
ACTIVITY NO.	ACTIVITY (FUNCTIONS)		

Figure 14-1. Activity list for work distribution chart.

Idle Time

In most functions there will be idle time, time for resting and delays, time awaiting work, and other nonproductive time in every day's work. Even in the most well-organized situation, an average of about one sixth of the available hours is lost through chatting, smoking, per-

NAME:	OCCUPATION or TITLE:	CLASSIFICATION:			
DEPARTMENT:	SECTION:	SUPERVISOR:	DATE:		
TASK NUMBER	DESCRIPTION		QUANTITY	POSTED TO ACTIVITY NO.	HOURS PER WEEK
			TOTAL		

Figure 14-2. Task list for distribution chart.

sonal needs, and all the other incidentals, such as dropping pencils on the floor, hanging up one's coat, having a cup of coffee, and so on. However, there are going to be a great many occasions when the majority of the staff (and doubtless the manager as well) has no clear idea how long different tasks will take. This is particularly the case in office situations where tasks are often interrupted and where, in some cases, several jobs are performed or attempted at once. In these cases a diary sheet or a tally form is usually the answer.

DIARY SHEET

The diary sheet is used in conjunction with the task list. From the specimen diary sheets, you will see that all that is done is that as one moves from one task to another, one puts the number of the ensuing task against the quarter-hour slot in which it was started. Interruptions and telephone calls are entered by tally marks, just as in the case of your own task list. The diary sheets are run for a sensible period of time. In a department that performs much the same work from one week to the next, a fortnight may well be sufficient to give a representative breakdown of the work. In other areas—for example, in an accounts department—the cycle might be monthly, and, therefore, the diary sheet will need to be run for a month. Occasionally there are areas where the cycle is of much longer duration than one month, but in these cases, one day per week on a staggered basis over the appropriate time period, for example, would provide a reasonable answer. Examples of diary sheets are given in Figures 14-3 and 14-4.

Reason for Diary Sheets

It is quite usual for staff people to make a mess of the first day's or the first two days' diary sheets through unfamiliarity, no matter how well you explain the situation. I would normally throw away the first two days and then use the subsequent ones for the analysis. Of course, one must explain fully to the employees why the diary sheets are being produced; employees should be told that they are not being timed personally or being asked to account for every minute of their day for future use in controlling them more tightly. When employees have a chance to demonstrate what they do, to demonstrate the complexity of their work, and to contribute to a study that might lead to better planning or more equitable distribution of work, they will normally be only too pleased to cooperate.

When the diary sheets have been completed, you should first re-

| Title .... | | | | | | Name .... | | |
| Date .... | | | | | | Dept. .... | | |

| Time | Item No. | Interruptions | | Quantities | Item No. | Description | Total Time | Total Unit | Unit Time |
		Phone	Other						
8:00						(as task list)			
:15									
:30									
:45									
9:00									
:15									
:30									
:45									
10:00									
:15									
:30									
:45									
11:00									
:15									
:30									
:45									
12:00									
:15									
:30									
:45									
1:00									
:15									
:30									
:45									
2:00									
:15									
:30									
:45									
3:00									
:15									
:30									
:45									
4:00						(Detail telephone and other interruptions here)			
:15									
:30									
:45									
5:00									
:15									
:30									
:45									
6:00									

Figure 14-3. Diary sheet.

Department:				Name:		Title:	Date:
Time	Item No.	Quantity		INTERRUPTIONS			
			Phone	Other	Details		
8:15							
:30							
:45							
9:00							
:15							
:30							
:45							
10:00							
:15							
:30							
:45							
11:00							
:15							
:30							
:45							
12:00							
:15							
:30							
:45							
1:00							
:15							
:30							
:45							
2:00							
:15							
:30							
:45							
3:00							
:15							
:30							
:45							
4:00							
:15							
:30							
:45							
5:00							
:15							
:30							
:45							
6:00							

Figure 14-4. Daily diary sheets (another example).

view the activity list and see whether the original analysis you made still stands. You should then transfer the activities, in the order of their importance, to the appropriate column in the work distribution chart.

WORK DISTRIBUTION CHART

An example of a work distribution chart is shown in Figure 14-5. You should review the task lists with the individual employees, and then set them in order of their importance—with your own list, if appropriate, on top. Then put your subordinates' names and other pertinent data on top of the work distribution chart, starting with yourself in the first column (if relevant), and then work from left to right. Of course, if additional columns are required, an extra sheet may be pasted on.

Now review each item on the task lists and enter the corresponding activity number, then transfer the separate tasks and hours to the space provided opposite the appropriate activity on the work distribution chart. You may, of course, combine two or more separate tasks listed by a subordinate into one task, but make sure that this task, with its activity number, is noted on the employee copy. If you are going to alter the hours shown on the task lists and diary sheets, it would be as well to discuss this with the subordinate concerned.

Clear and Full Picture Available

After all the hours and tasks have been recorded, add up the total hours both vertically and horizontally to show totals for each subordinate, the entire department, and each activity. Your chart now gives you a clear and full picture of your department and its work.

The information you have in front of you now on the work distribution chart is not completely accurate, nor is it work measurement in any classical sense of the term. What you have is a reasonably accurate and common-sense picture of the amounts of time that the department as a whole and the individuals involved spend on the different activities. This information can be used for three main purposes: for improvement, for cost evaluation, and for planning and control.

Figure 14-5. Work distribution chart.

ORGANIZATIONAL UNIT CHARTED: ....

Cha. by .... Apprd. by .... Chart Date ....

☐ PRESENT Covering ☐ Weeks
☐ PROPOSED diaries

(1) Name & (2) Position

NO.	ACTIVITIES (Functions) & TASKS (Jobs)	Quantities	TOT. HRS.	1	2	1	2	1	2	1	2	1	2	1	2	1	2	1	2	1	2	1	2	1	2	1	2	1	2	1	2	1	2	1	2
				HRS.	HRS.	HRS.	HRS.	HRS.	HRS.	HRS.	HRS.	HRS.	HRS.	HRS.	HRS.	HRS.	HRS.	HRS.	HRS.	HRS.	HRS.															

(Enter first activity, then all tasks related to that activity, then proceed to the next activity).

INSERT SUB-TOTALS
OR TOTALS (MANHOURS)

Improvement

Let us first take the question of improvement. Anyone can have a flash of inspiration, but most improvements in industrial and commercial organizations are obtained through the use of a disciplined approach to any data provided. One of these approaches is called critical analysis. In this we ask ourselves six questions about each major point in any data that are the subject of our investigation. The questions are: Why? What? Where? When? Who? and How?

Why and what? Having prepared our work distribution chart, we can first ask two questions, "why" and "what." We ask ourselves, *"Why* is this activity necessary? Is it properly a function?" Then we say, *"What* does this activity accomplish? Is it cost-effective, or is the amount of time shown a reasonable amount of time for this activity as a percentage of the whole?" We are going to go over each activity to see whether it makes sense to perform it at all and whether it is absolutely necessary or is duplicated by another department. We are going to determine if the activities are in keeping with the objectives of the department and, incidentally, whether the objectives of our department are in keeping with the needs of the company.

The second stage is to read horizontally across the chart and to look at one task at a time. For this step, we will use the questions "Where," "When," "Who," and "How."

Where? Where in the department or in the company should this task be done? Consider available skills, equipment, files, similar reports, the layout, and where similar work is done. Obviously one either wants to transfer the activity to the area where you have the least overall cost, or, if cost is not so important, where it will be conducted most efficiently.

When? In what part of the day, the week, or the month should this task be performed? Does it need rescheduling to balance the daily work load, or should it be batched to save a lot of preparation and putting elements away? When, in fact, is it required? Hourly, daily, weekly, or monthly? Or have we checked recently to find out whether our present deadlines coincide with the real requirements or whether, for example, half the data would be sufficient to get the next department started? Would an estimate, a projection, or a set of rounded figures do just as well?

Who? Who does this? Who has the skill needed? Who does something similar or duplicates it? Should anyone specialize? Who has the ability to cover, in case of sickness, absence, or a fluctuation in work?

How? How can be asked in two ways. One is to analyze each person independently and look at his job as a whole. How related are the tasks of this person to others? How are his skills utilized? Is he spending 5 percent of his time on something for which he is trained, and 95 percent of his time on some routine work that could be transferred elsewhere? How are his skills utilized? How repetitive are his tasks? How much checking or supervision is there? How many deadlines or monotonous tasks? How heavy is his work load? It is becoming more and more important to give people authority and responsibility in their work, to encourage interest in their jobs, and to give them a fair shake.

The other use of *how* is to ask, how it is performed? Except in the most simple operations, it is a good idea to do a simple block flow-chart or diagram of the main steps in a procedure. Examples are given in Figures 14-6 and 14-7. After you have prepared a block chart of the procedure, you can apply critical analysis to it again, since critical analysis always yields an additional set of results as one looks at each procedure in more detail.

There is nothing done so well that it cannot be done better—or more simply, or more sensibly. By applying the critical analysis sequence to different steps in the procedure, one will find that there are many activities that are unnecessary—or, if necessary, that are not cost-effective. Costs are changing all the time, particularly energy and labor costs, which have changed out of all proportion to other costs over the last few years. Assumptions made on the best evidence ten years ago may well not be valid today. In fact, who would say that *any* assumptions made ten years ago would have been made in the same way if they had been reached under present conditions? In most areas you will find habits and procedures that have been in operation for much longer than that.

Cost Evaluation

You will understand that if you have an analysis of the time taken for the various activities or procedures conducted in your area, and if you can know or assume the volumes or levels of business involved, then

Job: Preparing an estimate (present method).

Chart begins with drawing and schedule in the sales department
'Out' basket, and ends with the completed estimate in the
sales department 'In' basket

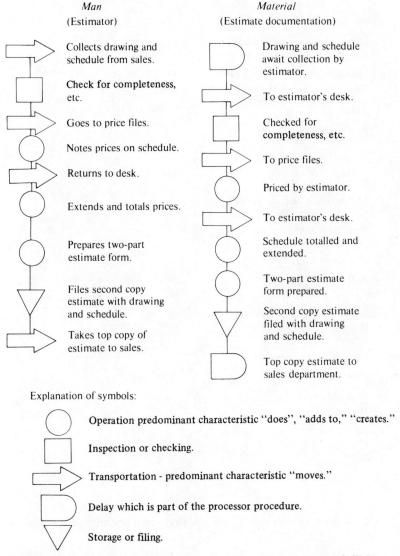

| *Man* | *Material* |
| (Estimator) | (Estimate documentation) |

Collects drawing and schedule from sales.

Check for completeness, etc.

Goes to price files.

Notes prices on schedule.

Returns to desk.

Extends and totals prices.

Prepares two-part estimate form.

Files second copy estimate with drawing and schedule.

Takes top copy of estimate to sales.

Drawing and schedule await collection by estimator.

To estimator's desk.

Checked for completeness, etc.

To price files.

Priced by estimator.

To estimator's desk.

Schedule totalled and extended.

Two-part estimate form prepared.

Second copy estimate filed with drawing and schedule.

Top copy estimate to sales department.

Explanation of symbols:

Operation predominant characteristic "does", "adds to," "creates."

Inspection or checking.

Transportation - predominant characteristic "moves."

Delay which is part of the processor procedure.

Storage or filing.

Figure 14-6. Flow process charts—"man"-type and "material"-type.

Storekeeper
1. Get goods for customer.
2. Check credit.
3. Make out invoice/delivery note and send to Accounts daily.

Accounts people–daily invoices
1. Account for invoice numbers.
2. Separate copies of invoice/delivery note and send Copy 2 to statistics 'for management information' and retain Copy 3.
3. Batch and add-list copies.

4. Select ledger card
5. If none, check new accounts list and make out ledger card.
6. If not on new accounts list see office manager.
7. Mail ledger card.
8. Mail control card.

Accounts people–cash received
1. If no cash advice included, make one.
2. List advices, list checks.
3. Compare and agree lists.
4. Bank checks.
5. Mail advices to ledger cards.

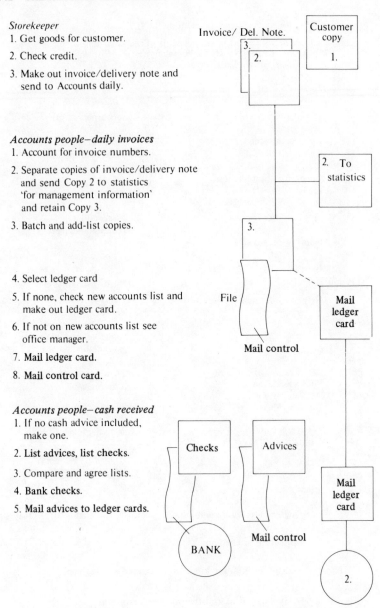

Figure 14-7. Flowchart of simple sales and account procedure.

you can put a cost on individual transactions; you will also have the information for producing a control form to make sure that you have the appropriate amount of labor to get the work done, as well as a means for forecasting your manpower requirements for the future.

Planning and Control

Chapter 16 describes methods of using these figures for manpower planning and labor control and goes into more detail about how to evaluate and account for the performance levels of your staff as they will be revealed by this kind of analysis.

Exercises

1. Calculate the variable and fixed costs of your department or function. If there are no management accounts, you can obtain a rough figure by multiplying the average salary by the number of employees and adding an estimate of the directly variable overheads. In low-overhead situations, this will be about 70 percent, ranging up to 120–130 percent in head offices. Fixed overheads can be taken globally and divided by the number of employees.
2. Calculate a cost-per-hour and cost-per-minute figure for each employee, bearing in mind holidays, sickness, and other absences.
3. If possible, calculate the cost in your department of each transaction, unit, batch, and so forth.
4. Draft task and activity lists for your area.

A man came to bathe in a river. He thought the water would be cool and refreshing. But instead he found an ocean with roaring waves. He was frightened.

15 Causes of Difference in Output

The manager does not want to waste the labor of his staff, one of the most expensive and scarce resources under his control. We all want to operate at maximum effectiveness by planning to keep our subordinates occupied with useful work. So, we have to assess the work content of our procedures, and we have to assess the capacity of our employees. Both may vary: the amount of work to be done will alter, and the output of our staff will change.

This chapter aims to provide a checklist of the factors that can cause a change in output or rate of working and that may explain differences in performance. To understand and plan the output of our staff, we will want to consider these factors, whether intuitively or systematically.

METHODS

It is generally found that incorrect methods are the main depressing influence on output. Under the heading of methods are included:

Layout
Workplace
Housekeeping
Procedures
Implementation of changes
Training in methods

In order to control the work of a section, department, or branch, we have to agree to a method for doing that work. Sometimes staff will improve on the specified method, but in general, departure from the method will involve additional elements of work which increase the time taken.

Layout and Workplace Organization

If performance falls below the expected level, the manager should check whether the layout and the workplace organization are as agreed to, and whether the "housekeeping" is as good as was envisaged. He should check whether there are any agreed-upon methods changes that have to be implemented. He should check whether the staff knows and follows the agreed-upon methods, and should consider whether he and his seniors are spending enough time in training the others in those methods.

Unnecessary Actions

He may find that unnecessary actions have crept in, or that work is being done over which there could be a difference of opinion. An example of this is "rechecking" references or calculations to "make sure." The manager must then decide if the rechecking serves a valid purpose—are errors picked up, and is the cost of those errors enough to justify the rechecking?

Other Determining Factors

If, however, the procedures and layout are substantially as agreed upon, the supervisor will have to look further. He may have been aware, of course, of other determining factors before he looked at the procedures. These will fall into two categories: other considerations affecting methods, and those that bear on the actual performance of the individual staff and on the section as a whole. The former are variations in quality of input, output, and materials.

Variations in the nature and quality of documents and source data. Such variations may or may not affect the detail of the procedures, but often affect the proportions of one element to another. In general, these variations would fall into one or more of the following categories, and these could be checked by sampling:

A different "mix"
Variation in form
Variation in content
Variation in legibility
Variation in error rate
Variation in flow

Quality of output. The same sort of considerations applies to the quality of output as to the quality of input. The quality of work in the section may go up or down, and while the basic procedures remain unchanged, the detailed methods will be found to have altered.

Variations in quality of materials. These can have a major effect in production and maintenance areas. It may well be that a change in supply or in buying specification occurred without the manager's being informed. Small changes in specification of office stationery and of consumables are less likely to be significant; changes such as those from carbon interleaving to snap-out sets for correspondence would fall into the category of methods changes; and, in the field of machine operation—particularly with printing, collating, and photocopying machines—a change in paper or materials may result in the equipment's being run at a higher speed than was previously accepted as normal. Less suitable materials would result, of course, in reduced performance. It should be noted that the supplier may have changed the specification, with or without notice, and the supervisor may not be aware of the change.

EFFORT

Even if the methods are correct, the required standard of effort, skill, or conditions may not be met. The manager should check

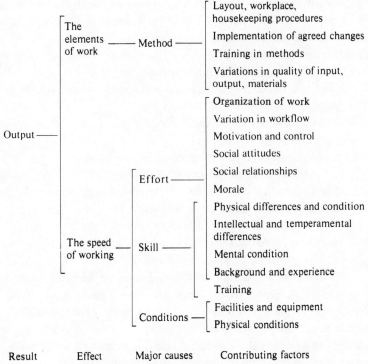

Result   Effect   Major causes   Contributing factors

Figure 15-1. Causes of difference in output.

the following points to see whether he needs to take action. (See Figure 15–1.)

Organization of Work

Recognition must be given to the fact that repetition of operations leads to different levels of speeds resulting from special skills, and that a higher average performance results when the staff can settle down to a regular repetitive operation (such as occurs, for example, on production lines).

In general, one cannot fully achieve this smooth rhythmic motion pattern that can be characteristic of the production line, but there may be opportunities for moving toward this kind of approach. By batching work, and by applying the principles of motion economy, very large improvements in productivity (frequently on the order of 50 percent) can be achieved. Likewise, it follows that if the work flow is such that the staff can never settle down to its tasks (and never know from one minute to the next what will happen), performance will suffer. Disorganization often results from interruptions or "queries."

Suggestions. The action to be taken will vary from situation to situation, but some suggestions are as follows:

1. Split up the work so that each worker can concentrate on one job for a worthwhile period.

2. Avoid general access to departmental staff from outside.

3. In the event of large quantities of outside calls or callers, detail the staff to deal with these (possibly in rotation) so as to leave the rest free to concentrate on other work. Do not have more outside phone points working than you wish to handle.

4. Discourage personal visits. Try to restrict access to the department to specified times or to specified conditions.

5. Try to batch "queries" and avoid lengthy searches while the caller waits. If proper call-back arrangements are made, a great deal of time can be saved. Internal queries should be by note if practicable, and a notepad and pencil suitably placed by the entrance to the department can be useful. (It is remarkable how many queries seem to answer themselves if the questioner tries to formulate the question in writing.)

6. Analyze the interruptions and try to have them dealt with at first hand by the most appropriate person. But try not to let yourself (the manager or supervisor) get bogged down in the role of a superior query clerk.

From a general point of view, the manager should attempt to determine the work content—and therefore the cost—of the operations, transactions, or procedure, as well as the average performance. If an appropriate work measurement scheme has been installed, this will make assessment simpler, but there are other methods such as sampling, estimating, and time logging (diary sheets), which can give a useful indication.

Raising performances. Performances above or below the average should be seen for what they are, and the reasons for variations should be sought and kept under review. Once the cost of below-average performance is determined, it is much easier to make decisions about the factors that may be causing it. The manager should be constantly striving to raise the performance in his area to an acceptable level by means of enthusiastic leadership, and by the removal of obstacles to even higher output by better methods and better practice.

Variation in Work Flow

The manager should make every effort to see that work is fairly distributed and that employees are not kept waiting for work. He will know that periods of inactivity are bad for morale, and that it may be difficult to restore a proper working tempo if there are too many gaps. We know that in certain circumstances unavoidable troughs will occur which cannot be filled by special jobs, temporary transfers, or other expedients. The manager should calculate the effect of these troughs as accurately as possible, and target accordingly (see also Chapter 6). At the very least, he will become aware of the cost and effects of the variability of the work flow and will be alive to any opportunities that develop for reducing that variability.

Motivation and Control

We see here a major role of the supervisor. It is most desirable to encourage delegation of authority and responsibility to the lowest practicable level, and it is equally important to be cost- and innovation-conscious, and fully in control of the work and the employees. Some of the underlying factors affecting personal output are discussed below.

Social Attitudes

Output will be affected by social attitudes in certain cases. Political attitudes can be important: for instance, a person who does not believe in the capitalist system will not have the same attitude to the commercial problems of the enterprise as one who is convinced of the necessity of competition and the profit motive. Someone who believes the economy is sound and expanding will view change and effort differently from one who sees it as static or declining. Likewise, a highly religious or sensitive person may recoil from hard-nosed purchasing and selling work or bad-debt recovery procedures. Traditionalists may be upset if, for example, personal letters are replaced by a stereotyped form.

History. History plays a part, too. In an area where unemployment, business crashes, or rapid hiring and firing have been experienced, people will react differently than they would in a place where respectable and prosperous employers have competed for the available labor for as long as anyone can remember. The history of the company itself will also play an important part.

Constructive and confident attitude. The manager must adopt a constructive and confident attitude, and should attempt to reconcile the individuals' view with his work and with the policy of the company or organization. He should be ready to demonstrate the relevance of the work to the future of the individual, group, company, community, or country as appropriate. This enthusiasm will eventually rub off on the others, and, even if he makes no converts, employees will respect him better if they feel he understands their beliefs and feelings and is prepared to discuss them.

Groups. Groups are not the same as individuals. Groups will adopt certain attitudes and tempos of work, and their members will tend to conform when they are in the group situation. You should consider whether there will be an improvement in making it possible for troublemakers and misfits to be transferred to where they would be more useful.

Morale. Morale is an amalgam of all the points mentioned in this chapter. We believe that if staff people can be shown that they are playing a valuable part in a successful and respected enterprise, and that they are using their talents in the best way to benefit both themselves and their employer, they will respond remarkably well.

Remember also that after one has been in any company for a few years, it becomes only too easy to see the last-minute panics, the shifts and devices, the personal failings, and the mistakes. The thing is to keep on trying; at least you will win some of the time.

Personal differences. One would expect that in an organization with proper selection procedures, wage structures, and job-grading and promotion arrangements, the staff recruited will be of at least average caliber and will be trained and placed in a satisfactory manner.

Quality of employees. However, even allowing for a percentage of mistakes, one is often surprised at how many complaints are made about the quality of employees. Sometimes this is a case of the bad worker blaming his tools (there are no bad men, only bad officers). A manager who criticizes his staff may well be really saying, "I am unable to get these people to do what I want." Perhaps there are also few really bad officers, but many managers and supervisors do not have sufficient training—they do not have the tools for the job, and it is the aim of this book to help in this respect.

Social Relationships and Behavior

We have considered the effect of various factors and relationships on individual members of the staff. We know that the individuals' needs for recognition and inclusion are affected by their relationships with:

> Other staff
> Supervision
> Management
> Family
> Other people outside the company

Behavior of people. What is surprising sometimes, however, is the apparent contradiction between the behavior of a person when he is on his own and when he is in a group—for example, at a meeting. This can be quite confusing, as, for instance, when a person privately accepts a proposed change and then publicly argues against it later, or, alternatively, when he refuses to have anything to do with a certain line of thinking and then warmly supports it at the meeting. Often this may be no more than a subconscious or only partly deliberate device to gain time to sort the matter out or to discuss it elsewhere. Sometimes it may be a question of positions: the manager, foreman, supervisor, or staff may have adopted a certain position on the procedures or operation of the section, and they all may feel that they cannot go back on this in front of each other without suffering a loss of face. Sometimes they may feel that they have to assert themselves by taking a certain line that is contrary to their own reasoning. In situations where the natural nervousness or diffidence of an individual is brought out, he may retreat from a proposal that he is not absolutely certain about.

Staff as a group. The same sort of considerations apply in dealing with the staff as a group—for example, in talks or discussions. Most groups subconsciously create a spokesman, and this person can be most useful in gaining the staff's cooperation. Obviously the foreman or supervisor is the local spokesman, but he has to work on the situation as he finds it.

Leadership. A leader uses example, persuasion, and compulsion to make people do what they would otherwise be uninclined or unable to do. Leadership involves an understanding of people, their strengths and weaknesses, and their hopes and fears, and we will now attempt to summarize these factors so that we can know better why individuals perform and act in different ways.

Physical Differences

Physical differences and physical skills are more important in manual working situations. Most office work requires no special physical effort or abilities and, given training, normal differences of age, sex, physique, and left- and righthandedness, are not too significant in themselves. Extremes of age and youth or dexterity and clumsiness would affect results, but the manager should have no difficulty in recognizing this.

Disabled or handicapped persons. Disabled or handicapped persons are at a disadvantage, although this can often be minimized, such as by giving a legless man a completely sedentary job. By law (the Rehabilitation Act of 1973 and the Vietnam-Era Veterans Readjustment Assistance Act of 1974), job discrimination against disabled persons is forbidden on federally funded projects, and affirmative-action standards are set up for all government contractors and subcontractors. Many states and municipalities have similar statutes.

Just as in the case of trainees, the supervisor will determine what he can expect, and will target accordingly. He should not demand that handicapped persons produce at the same level as "normal" employees, but he should expect an appropriate amount of production (although in some jobs, handicapped persons' very lack of mobility and their greater motivation to do the job well will make them even more productive than the average employee). In any case, it should be made clear to all such persons that none of them would be pressed to perform at more than their capacity. Most supervisors know that it is counterproductive to ask too much of *any* of their subordinates.

Physical Condition

Physical condition in employees is important. It is not necessary for them to be athletically "fit" (this may even be a disadvantage in a sedentary occupation), but workers should be reasonably fresh and alert throughout the day. Unfitness leads to absence, laziness, and often a grudging attitude to work. Physical condition may be affected by ventilation, lighting, cramped conditions, and other things that are within the employer's control.

Other factors which affect fitness for work include:

1. Moonlighting (evening and weekend jobs).
2. Excessive social commitments (particularly with young people).
3. Heavy domestic commitments (for example, children, moving house, looking after relatives, and marital difficulties).
4. Outside activities (charity work, service on the school board).
5. Difficult commuting.
6. Alcoholism.
7. Inadequate feeding. Women on staff sometimes skip breakfast and have a small lunch. This can lead to loss of concentration in the afternoon.

The company may have a policy on these points and on bad attendance records, but in general the manager can only accept these factors and judge accordingly (in his official capacity, at least).

Intellectual and Temperamental Differences

It can be useful to realize that there are intellectual and temperamental differences in people and to use this knowledge in harnessing their abilities in the most effective way. It may help to understand apparently inexplicable contradictions in behavior and performance. It is not within the compass of this book to consider in detail the range of temperamental and intellectual make-up, but, as with physical characteristics, otherwise suitably equipped persons can be reduced to a low level of performance and concentration if they are not mentally fit.

Mental Condition

We cannot go into the question of mental breakdowns or disorders of the mind and of the nervous system, although the incidence of this kind of illness is increasing. It may be possible to see that something is wrong, because the person suffers a deep depression or behaves as if he is "off his rocker." What we are much more likely to encounter is:

1. *Preoccupation.* Worries over domestic problems (such as spouse, sweetheart, children, or money) will all distract people.

2. *Shock.* Tragic experiences like deaths or seeing an accident may throw employees off their form for a period.

3. *Tiredness.* This is linked with the points of physical fitness. A tired body can house an alert mind and vice versa, but generally a lack of mental energy will accompany a lack of physical energy.

Background and Experience

The extent to which an individual can control and direct his mental abilities and temperamental characteristics is greatly influenced by background, education, and experience. The basic mental horsepower or I.Q. of the individual does not develop much after the age of 16, but powers of concentration, flexibility of approach, and development of mental abilities can be improved until the individual is in his forties or fifties. In many cases a person who can make good use of a limited I.Q. can put in a better performance than a person who has a higher I.Q. but less mental discipline. In clerical work one must match the individual to the work: too good a mind will get frustrated and dull; too limited an intelligence will be strained.

Training

One of the most obvious causes of differences in output is the degree and quality of training and of experience. Targeting of performance will be set by the manager and supervisor in the light of this, and they will be aware of the cost of staff turnover on the one hand and of the necessity for careful training on the other.

By demonstration, and by using whatever aids he can obtain or produce (for example, charts, diagrams, and checklists), the manager will ensure that each employee understands the agreed-upon methods and procedures in detail, and will watch to see that these procedures are followed (until better ones are developed). See Chapter 13 for a discussion of teaching and training methods.

It need hardly be said that short-interval schedule figures and standards (where available) can be a valuable aid in assessing the progress of trainees.

CONDITIONS

Facilities and Equipment

It is well to check the following points:

1. Are furniture and fixtures of proper height and size? Are they limiting the work in any way?
2. Is there enough space for orderly storage?
3. Do drawers and doors open properly or do they interfere with other operations?
4. Are the seats properly adjusted and comfortable?
5. Is all equipment functioning properly? Are there suitable maintenance arrangements?
6. Do the key staff people understand the use of the equipment?
7. Are materials and tools placed for easiest access and disposal?

Physical Conditions

Physical conditions and environment will affect the rate of working and, in some cases, the methods. Good work performances can be obtained in all except extreme conditions, but the following points should be noted.

Light. Natural light should fall over the left shoulder or come from the left (for right-handed operations), and staff should not face a window. Direct or reflected glare and excessive variations in brightness should be avoided. A higher level of illumination is required for machine work.

Heat. The temperature should be controlled within the range allowed by federal energy-conservation rules.

Ventilation. Poor ventilation will lead to concentration of carbon dioxide in the air and to sleepy and unhealthy conditions. Odors and smoke should be cleared without causing drafts.

Noise. Most people can get used to a steady hum, but are distracted by intermittent noise. A high noise level is tiring and can be reduced by acoustic tiling, screening, doubleglazing, and soft floor coverings— for example, cork tiles or carpets.

Space. In most expanding companies, space is in short supply, as well as being expensive, but workers do feel better when they can move freely about and do not feel hemmed in at their places of work. Supervision, too, is easier in areas that are laid out with more than the bare minimum of space.

Environment. The general standard of decor, machines, equipment and furniture, and of rest room, cloakroom, canteen, parking facilities, and the like will often fall outside the immediate responsibility of the manager, although these matters will almost certainly be raised by the employees. The manager may attend meetings or have other occasions in which he can put forward recommendations about these things, either on his own or in conjunction with other people.

The manager cannot measure the effect of poor environment or physical conditions, but he can know that changes in them will cause differences in output. He should acquire copies of the relevant legislation concerning physical conditions.

Performance

We have considered a wide variety of factors that could lead to performance's falling below (or in rarer cases, exceeding) a reasonable standard. Many of these factors are of vital interest to management and supervision in a wider context than work performances. Most of them imply a requirement of personal knowledge of people and of the work situation in each section, which is in itself probably the first step to achieving effective management.

Exercises

1. Identify three occasions on which output has varied from what you expected. Attempt to analyze the reasons for this.

2. Identify one member of your staff who produces better results than you would have expected. What are the reasons for this, and would they be relevant to any other people?

3. Identify one member of your staff who produces worse results than he should. What are the reasons for this, and can you do anything about them? Might these factors affect any other staff people?

4. Are there any occasions when you feel you cannot give your best? Why is this, and would the reasons be applicable to any other staff people? Is this likely to happen more or less frequently?

"You always rise twice," he said, "is no consolation to a man that thinks to drown."   A. L. ROWSE

16 Manpower Planning and Control

In chapter 14 we looked at a simple method of obtaining a ratio or relationship between the work to be done and the labor required. There are various ways of doing this, and this chapter assumes that you have obtained this basic information and want to consider ways of using it for planning and control.

PERFORMANCE AND PROGRESS REPORT

There are various forms that can be used; a very common one is known as the performance and progress report. A more complex version of this form, which can assist in manpower planning, is given in Figure 16–1.

Mechanics of the Form

Basis of plan. The mechanics of the preparation of this form are as follows. In the "basis of plan" box, put in the company plan, marketing plan, or source data, which may be estimates from an examination of historical figures that you used to look ahead in planning your manpower.

Volume. Under the column "volume," we would enter the activities as determined in producing the work distribution chart in lines 1 to 9. (If there are more than nine operations, obviously one would use additional sheets or a form designed with more lines on it.) Then enter the forecast volumes of all operations by period, and add all lines across to give annual totals.

Unit time. Periods will vary from company to company as appropriate, depending on the accounting or management information arrangements. In some cases, it may be by calendar month; in other cases, by four-week periods or quarters. Under the "unit time" column, insert the time needed for each procedure or transaction or unit as established from the work distribution chart. If you have not already done this, all that is required is to divide the total time (for example, that spent on processing invoices) by the number of invoices processed during the period. Then multiply the volumes by the times for each period, rounding to the nearest hour. Add these up to give period-totals of hours. If more than one sheet has to be used, total all sheets and carry forward the totals to sheet 1, then enter these figures on part two of the form.

Hours required. In the last section of the form, which is described as "hours required," there are three sections. One is hours required for regular work; another, for any special work, such as budget preparation, year-end accounts, or inventory. Sometimes you may wish to add extra hours for service levels—for example, in the case of a bank, a check-in area, or a booking office, where it may be necessary to provide a greater number of clerks in order to facilitate an acceptable level of service, regardless of the actual amount of work.

The amount of work will fluctuate during the year, and obviously it is one of the purposes of the exercise to quantify this variation. The performance of people against the differing volumes should normally be a constant ratio, except where there are seasonal effects on the characteristics of the work. In the latter case, there may be two or more levels of performance during the year, but periodic variations in work volumes should not in themselves cause fluctuations in the unit times. What can occur, however, is an improvement or deterioration in the level of performance for other reasons.

Part 1. Output. Page ..... of .....   Division/Dept. ....   Branch ....   Section ....

Basis of plan

Activity	Volume	Unit time	PERIOD 1		PERIOD 2		PERIOD 3		PERIOD 4		PERIOD 5		PERIOD 6		TOTAL
			Planned	Actual	Planned	Actual	Planned	Actual	Planned	Actual	Planned	Actual	Planned	Actual	
1.															
2.															
3.															
4.															
5.															
6.															
7.															
8.															
9.															
Activity															
1.															
2.															
3.															
4.															
5.															
6.															
7.															
8.															
9.															
Subtotal															
B/F from page															
Total															
Man-hours required															
Regular work															
Special work															
Service work															
Total															
Adjustments made to performance level, if any															
+ %															
− %															

Figure 16-1. Manpower plan.

Part 2. Input. Page   of   Division/Dept................   Branch...............Section............

C. Proposed number of staff	PERIOD 1		PERIOD 2		PERIOD 3		PERIOD 4		PERIOD 5		PERIOD 6		TOTAL
	Planned	Actual	Planned	Actual	Planned	Actual	Planned	Actual	Planned	Actual	Planned	Actual	
Permanent													
Temporary													
Total													
Supervision													

D. Man-hours provided	PERIOD 1		PERIOD 2		PERIOD 3		PERIOD 4		PERIOD 5		PERIOD 6		TOTAL
	Planned	Actual	Planned	Actual	Planned	Actual	Planned	Actual	Planned	Actual	Planned	Actual	
Permanent staff:													
(i) - holiday													
(ii) - sickness													
(iii) - leave													
(iv) - training													
(v) Subtotal													
(vi) loaning out													
(vii) + borrowing													
(viii) + overtime													
Temporary staff:													
(ix) Net staff													
Hours required (from Part 1)													
Surplus													
+ leave													
Maximum leave capability													

Figure 16-1. Part 2.

Effective utilization of time. When some sort of control or target is applied to the actual effectiveness of the staff, then effective utilization of time normally improves. It is impossible to be specific about this, but the general situation in an "uncontrolled" area is that performances are something like 60 percent of optimum; by the use of the type of techniques mentioned in the book, and by controls, one can increase productivity by 20 or 30 percent. It follows that any movement in that direction would influence the calculations involved in estimating the requirement for future periods or months.

The next step is to determine the basic permanent staff numbers, and you will need to use part two of your manpower planning form. The object of this is to match, as closely as possible, the net staff hours shown at the bottom of the section "man-hours provided" with the hours required from the bottom of part one. There will be a degree of trial and error before the final level of staff and overtime can be determined.

Man-hours Provided

A base figure is required to start the calculations. Enter this at the top, extend it to give the permanent staff gross attendance hours in each period, and enter these figures on the first line of the "man-hours provided" section. (The present or expected permanent staff numbers multiplied by the normal working hours per period will give the gross attendance hours.)

Permanent staff—public holidays. In addition to annual leave, public holidays should be added in the appropriate period.

Permanent staff—sickness. Estimate expected absence through sickness, taking into account likely seasonal variations, and enter these in the appropriate periods. Average sickness per employee in excess of two weeks per year should be recorded as worthy of further investigation.

Annual leave. Enter expected or planned figures.

Training program. Enter expected or planned figures.

Subtotal. Deduct holidays, sickness, annual leave, and training from permanent staff attendance hours. The resulting balance, at this point in the completion of the forms, will give the present anticipated provision of permanent staff time, period by period. These figures should be compared with the period totals of required hours to show shortfalls or exercises requiring adjustment in the following manner.

Training and leave. The first step toward obtaining any extra time on a period-by-period basis is to consider whether any training or leave, at present allocated in periods where shortfalls occur, can be further regulated. Make any possible adjustments and compare to see whether shortfalls still exist.

Borrowing and lending of time. The next step is to explore with the other managers the availability of surplus staff time in other sections or branches having appropriate skills. In the event that arrangements can be made to borrow time, enter the amounts for each period. Separate lines can be used to show sections from which the time has been borrowed. If there is a surplus in your own function, then the reverse process should be adopted.

Temporary staff. If the time made available by borrowing does not meet the shortfall, or if borrowing is not practicable, the possibility of recruiting temporary staff for the required periods should be considered, and if arrangements can be made, the time they will contribute should be entered in the appropriate line.

Overtime. Any remaining shortfalls should be met by overtime to the extent that local agreements allow, and only as far as is reasonable—and, of course, provided that the economics are workable and demonstrable. However, if at this stage it is apparent that the shortfalls in any period or periods cannot be met practically and economically by borrowed time, temporary staff, and overtime, it then becomes necessary to go back to the beginning of the first section and to draw up a new plan on the basis of additional staff numbers. This may, of course, include either permanent employees or seasonal and part-time workers recruited at the appropriate time to meet needs. These extra people should be added only to the extent necessary to reach the minimum of man-hours required after borrowing and when the use of temporary staff people and overtime opportunities have been fully explored.

Addition of columns. The addition of the columns will now give planned net staff hours available, and these should again be compared with the period totals of required hours to show any surplus hours available. If there are surplus hours, then these should be offered as far as practicable to the other sections or branches in the organization or they should be used for any other necessary work (subject to the considerations outlined in the next paragraph). If arrangements are made to lend any surplus time, enter the amounts period by period. Separate lines can be used to show the sections to which staff has been loaned. Then complete the period columns to give net attendance hours and add all lines across to give annual totals.

Monthly Surpluses

At the bottom of the form are columns for monthly surpluses. It may be necessary and desirable to have some surplus in reserve to provide for the effects of partly trained staff, disabled staff, temporary fluctuations, or for any other reason. However, this figure should not be too high, since the figures obtained from the work distribution chart represent levels of effectiveness related to the present situation.

Planning and Scheduling Purposes

The completed form and the figures obtained from the work distribution chart can also be used for planning and scheduling purposes, and Chapter 6 should be considered in conjunction with results at this time. You have now a valuable tool to assist in short-term staff planning and control. You have a means of justifying staff increases (or decreases) against estimated or actual changes in work load and business volumes.

MONTHLY PERFORMANCE CONTROL SHEET

By now, you will appreciate that the form and system can be extended in detail, or can be modified to show a variety of figures to help you in the management of your function. Examples of monthly "control" sheets are given in Figures 16-2, 16-3, and 16-4.

Although this exercise of the preparation of manpower plan is valuable, it takes little account of the "people" as distinct from the requirements of the work, and a detailed approach of this kind could not be applied for more than a few months into the future. The problem of longer-term manpower and succession planning can be looked at from an entirely different standpoint, and this is done by taking a "stock" or

Department .... Month ....

Section .... Year ....

		Function/Task	Basis of assessment	Time	Month units	Time × units
MAN HOURS PROVIDED*	1. Permanent					
	2. Temporary					
	3. Borrowing					
	4. Overtime					
	5. TOTAL					
HOURS PAID FOR BUT NOT WORKED	Holidays					
	Sickness					
	Leave					
	Training					
	Other					
	6. TOTAL					
	7. Net hours worked (5–6)					
HRS PD BUT NOT SPENT ON MEASD WORK	8. Loaned out					
	9. Special jobs (Unplanned or unexpected work)					
	10. Net hours on normal work (7−(8+9))					
	11. Net hours on measured wk % of total hours $\left(\frac{10\times100}{5}\right)$					
	12. Workload (Total of final column)					
	13. Variance (12 X 10)					
	14. EFFECTIVENESS $\left(\frac{12 \times 100}{10}\right)$					
	15. Staff numbers					
	16. Supervision					
	17. Staff					

*Code figures refer to column numbers in the performance and progress report

Figure 16-2. Monthly performance control sheet.

JOB SUMMARY OF STANDARD HOURS

DEPARTMENT   DATE

1 POSITION AND FUNCTIONS	2 BASIS OF MEASUREMENT	3 Unit Time	4 Actual Units	5 Work Hours	6 Actual Hours	7 Variance	8 % Effective
—	—	—	—	3×4	—	$6-5$	$\frac{5}{6} \times 100$
		(Time for transaction or procedure)					

Figure 16-3. Another example of a control sheet.

"inventory" of one's people, and then comparing this with the company's requirements at different points in the future.

LONGER-TERM PLANNING

The approach detailed next can be used for somewhere between 300 and 800 people at a maximum, because for larger numbers it is necessary to have a computer or other equipment facilitate the movement of the data required. The approach must be modified to meet individual circumstances, but what is suggested is in essence as follows. Examine the jobs or positions in the organization or the senior posts in your own area. Once you have set out the situation in terms of job titles and numbers, consider the kind of requirements needed for filling those various posts. Then look at the number of people you employ who are already in your area, and consider whether they have the requirements to fill not only the positions they are already filling, but also more senior posts. When you have done this, complete a matrix. An example of a manpower planning matrix is shown in Figure 16-5.

You will see that the matrix is set out in terms of the individuals' ages, because this is the one sure thing in all manpower planning—the inexorable (and regrettable!) march year by year toward retirement age. The matrix is also divided into male and female, because the career pattern and expectations of women are still different, even in this age of equal opportunity.

Other matrixes can be made up for future years and situations, but for a quick look, all one has to do is run a ruler down from the top of the matrix to blank out those who will have been lost to retirement in one to five years' time, or whatever the period selected; you can compare what remains with the expected requirement established for the year concerned. This may be the same as now, but it may be expanded or reduced in expectation of the growth or attrition of the organization.

You can see now whether any serious gaps in age structure are likely to occur or whether there will be specific skills missing. You can look at the likely career progression of groups and individuals, and also forecast your own prospects. (It is normal to obtain a clearer and more favorable view of the opportunities that are likely to turn up

Figure 16-4. Example of a summary control sheet.

Company _____ Department _____ Section _____ Sheet No. _____

Month and Year 19......	Man-hours provided. Permanent (1)	Temporary (2)	Borrowed (3)	Overtime (4)	Hrs. not worked (deduct) (6)	Net hrs. worked (7)	Loaned (deduct) (8)	Special jobs (deduct) (9)	Net hrs. used on normal work (10)	Net hrs. on normal work as % of total net hrs. wkd. (11)	Workload (Times × units) (12)	Variance (13)	Effectiveness (14)	Current staff numbers Supervision (16)	Staff (17)	Any relevant comments
1																
2																
3																
4																
5																
6																
7																
8																
9																
10																
11																
12																
13																

MANPOWER PLANNING MATRIX — For period _____ Ref: _____ Prepared by _____ Date _____

AGE	*TIER I			*TIER II			*TIER III			*TIER IV			*TIER V			Total
	M	F	T	M	F	T	M	F	T	M	F	T	M	F	T	
64																
63																
62																
61																
60																
59																
58																
57																
56																
55																
54																
53																
52																
51																
50																
49																
48																
47																
46																
45																
44																
43																
42																
41																
40																

MANPOWER PLANNING MATRIX — For period _____ Ref: _____ Prepared by _____ Date _____

AGE	*TIER I			*TIER II			*TIER III			*TIER IV			*TIER V			Total
	M	F	T	M	F	T	M	F	T	M	F	T	M	F	T	
39																
38																
37																
36																
35																
34																
33																
32																
31																
30																
29																
28																
27																
26																
25																
24																
23																
22																
21																
20																
19																
18																
17																
16																
Totals																

*Note—"Tiers" are levels of ability or potential ability to fill different grades or ranks.

Figure 16-5. Manpower planning matrix.

through doing this sort of exercise.) However, the analysis, conclusions, and use of these approaches will vary considerably from individual to individual depending on circumstances. What was intended in this chapter was to show two different mechanisms for producing base data for further analysis or managerial thinking, and for taking action to manage your department in a better way.

Exercise

This chapter requires much thought on your part. The exercise is to consider how the control and planning of your major resource—manpower—can be of value in your situation, and then to set about doing it.

An action or work plan is set out in the summary chapter.

Verbal agreements aren't worth the paper they're written on.   SAM GOLDWYN

17 The Manager and the Trade Unions

The manager is expected to be good at everything; he is expected to cope with a variety of relationships and pressures, from directors and customers. This includes matters of profit and loss, income, costs, plant and equipment, and government legislation. In particular he has to deal with his subordinates, and in many cases, this involves contact and negotiation with union officials. This aspect of this task can often take up a major proportion of his time—time which he may grudge, since it takes him away from the many other matters with which he should be coping. What can he do about it? How can the manager handle all his duties and responsibilities in the face of pressures that often conflict?

I think it can be taken as axiomatic not only that unions are here to stay, but also that groups of employees not hitherto unionized will become so. It can also be accepted that the unions themselves will become better organized and more effective, and that local representatives will be better directed and trained. Whether subsequent governments like it or not, the power derived from the ability to withhold labor in vital situations will have to be accepted as part of our national structure.

SHOP STEWARDS

The manager is not normally confronted by "the union"; he is faced with the local official or shop steward. Shop stewards, as we shall call them, fall into three categories. First, they are people with some managerial instincts and drive who have failed for one reason or another to become, or to attempt to become, managers themselves. These people find an outlet for their need for success and responsibility in union work. Secondly, they are people who are dedicated to the union and its ideals, and who really enjoy this type of work. Thirdly, they consist of reluctant heroes, people who are elected to the position because nobody else will take it or because their colleagues want them to be there. Some would say that there is a fourth category consisting of people who find it easier to do union work than to get on with the tasks they were originally hired to do, but I think this is a small and declining percentage.

The manager should identify which kind of shop steward he has to deal with, but should always recognize that the union man is there to do a job and deserves as much courtesy and respect as any other colleague. The union official is a human being, and if he can withdraw your labor on one hand, or assist in the contribution of that labor on the other, then he is a very important person.

The shop steward is not subject to the same complex of pressures as the manager, and he does not require anything like the same abilities and training. But because he is concentrating on a few key tasks, basically protecting the rights of his members and securing as large a share of the cake as he can for them, he can be a formidable opponent. He may also be highly trained in negotiations to a superior level than the manager.

Pressures on Shop Stewards and Union Officials

You have attempted to find out what caliber of person the shop steward is. Be sure also to evaluate the pressures on him, from his branch or committee, from his members (often very strong), and from his own ego. A union leader's only criterion of success is what he achieves for his members. He has a strong personal need to strive for what they want and always to be pressing for something else—even if, as is often the case, and in times of government-backed norms and wage ceilings, it is increased security and better treatment rather than just more money and benefits that workers are looking for.

Profitability and Communication

Some unions employ their own productivity experts who will point to ways in which profitability can be maintained or improved at the same time that wage levels are raised.

The stewards can be invaluable as a means of communication and negotiation with the workforce, and in policing fair personnel policies. If management and supervisors work with them and not against them, union representatives can be good friends and sterling members of the industrial community.

INDUSTRIAL ACTION

However, in any human situation there will come a day when somebody says the wrong thing or breaks the rules, or when management and union cannot agree. Where is the manager, then? The steward can cause various disruptions, and these are, progressively:

Overtime bans
Strict (and therefore obstructive) compliance with the rule book
Slowdowns
Wildcat strikes
Official strikes

How did they happen? The most frequent cause of industrial action is lack of communication, whether real or imagined, but other causes are:

Differentials in pay
Higher pay at other companies

Work study rates
Conditions
Discipline

PROCEDURE AGREEMENT

Get some order into the situation. Arrive at a local or domestic procedural agreement with the union. This will be a comprehensive document that will lay down the rules for action in any industrial situation, whether over grievances, disputes, disciplinary procedures, or claims.

The agreement will have to conform to the provisions of federal, state, and local laws, and you may need to obtain legal advice on the application of some of these statutes to your own situation. The agreement will set out the reasons for industrial discipline, and it will define the relationships of the foreman, the management levels, the shop steward, and workers. In particular, it will define the relationships and authority of the foreman, who is the primary representative of the company's policy on the shop floor, and who is normally involved in the first stages of any disciplinary actions and disputes with stewards and workers.

There is not enough space in a book of this nature to include a specimen agreement, and in any case what would be appropriate in one situation might be inappropriate in another—for example, in matters of pay and seniority. However, all agreements will define the position regarding misconduct such as damage, stealing, constant bad timekeeping, drinking, and aggressive behavior, and at what point these transgressions merit oral and written warnings and dismissal, by whom this can be done, and what arrangements there may be for appeal.

Grievance Section

All agreements should have a grievance section, with a definition of grievances, a procedure and time scale for dealing with them, and an agreement not to stop work over a dispute until the grievance procedure has been exhausted.

Grievances include violations of the agreement, violation of safety laws or of other legislation, and unjust treatment. Violations of the agreement might comprise arguments over seniority, overtime rates, job reclassification, transfers, replacements, promotions, and pay scales. Unjust treatment of an employee might comprise matters such as personal discrimination, favoritism, excessive disciplining, and punishment for violation of unposted rules.

A typical grievance clause in an agreement reads as follows: "Grievance procedures may be instituted by an employee who alleges that he has been dealt with unfairly. Grievances may also be lodged by an employee who alleges that the provisions of this contract have not been complied with." Grievances should be lodged in writing and on a proper form. A sample form is shown in Figure 17-1, but all forms should include: a brief description of the case; a reference to the section of the agreement which is violated (if any); and the settlement

Name of Aggrieved employee ______________________ Time Card No. __________

Dept./Section ______________________________________

Employee's statement of grievance ______________________________________

Signature of employee ______________________ Signature of steward ______________

Date presented to foreman ____ /____ /____ Department ______________

Foreman's answer ______________________________________

Date ______________________ Signature of foreman ______________

Date to grievance committee ____ /____ /____ Chairman ______________

Figure 17-1. Grievance form.

wanted. The union may submit a grievance on its own behalf, and the shop steward or foreman may assist the employee in completing the form.

No agreement can cover every eventuality, although it can include a statement of policy as to treatment of matters not covered, and as to matters reserved entirely to management. Agreements should be "fair"—that is, not pressing too heavily on the employees, nor yet giving them too much leverage *vis-à-vis* the company and their supervisors. Agreements must be signed by the company and all unions involved; otherwise, they will not be considered valid by an industrial tribunal, and they must be renewed regularly and re-signed, possibly as each yearly wage bargaining is negotiated.

WAYS TO AVOID POSSIBLE CONFRONTATIONS

So what do we do to try to avoid getting caught in a situation where we have allowed unreasonable requests to arise, and where we have, as an alternative to a costly and nerve-wracking dispute, loss of face and an expensive and precedent-creating capitulation?

Joint Consultation Procedure

Keep in touch by having a joint consultation procedure whereby material changes in conditions, machinery, and systems can be discussed with the stewards, and where impending complaints and claims can be brought up by the union side. These meetings can provide an opportunity for improvement in communications, such as when the company's progress and future plans can be presented and discussed. Consultation meetings should be held at least quarterly, and there should be a provision for either side to request an emergency meeting.

Sensible or Fair Pay Structure

Job evaluation and grading systems which are clearly understood and accepted are a major factor in avoiding industrial troubles. An experienced negotiator suggested that the best way is to fix the top and bottom pay on the basis of market considerations, and then to let the grading committee (on which the management side should be a minority) sort out what happens in between.

Agreement on Security of Employment

The specter of redundancies, layoffs, short time, or firings of any kind increases the existing distrust between labor and management—as well it might. Perhaps you cannot guarantee perpetual employment, but at least you'll have the kind of clear, written agreement about the proper consultations and procedures that covers what would happen if there was a major downturn in business or a change in plans.

Policy on Pay and Productivity

Many disputes over pay arise because management has made no clear (or open) plans for increasing pay and other benefits. Considerable thought is given to improving profitability and productivity, but little to how much of the cake is being passed out. Labor learns that the only way to get a pay raise is to ask for one, and then to follow that soon after with threats and action. A Pavlovian response is created: no strike = small increase; strike = bigger increase. Perhaps the average, moderate union member does not want to strike for many reasons. (It not only hurts the company; it also hurts his pocketbook while it happens.) But he begins to learn that only by screwing management can he get a reasonable deal.

Decide on Your Objectives

In any negotiation over wages and working conditions, management should have in mind what it is prepared to pay and to concede that before starting. This final situation may well be expressed as a number of alternatives (such as basic pay, overtime, holiday and shift allowances, working hours, breaks, and productivity deals). The company will not offer all alternatives at the outset, just as the union will probably make initial claims in excess of the figure it feels it would finally settle for. This is the normal process of any bargaining, and, as each side adjusts to the other, a compromise is reached which is seen as the best that could be obtained under the circumstances. It is important for management to avoid a position in which either side has no further flexibility, one in which union negotiators backed by an angry committee and angry members feel that there is no point in continuing talks and that they must proceed to industrial action. Try always to explain why the company is taking a particular line or offering a particular figure.

WHEN DISPUTES OCCUR

These things will help, but there will still be disputes. When money is the subject, you can never satisfy everyone, and somebody at some point is bound to make a mistake. But when it comes to the showdown, remember a few points.

Always Tell the Truth

Respect any agreements and try not to make deals regarding their provisions. If the company is in the wrong, admit it, back down, and apologize. If there is some doubt, it may be better to give in than to see the business halted, but one should not give in over everything. If an issue is clear-cut, and if there is no serious risk in taking a stand at a particular time, fight and win your fight. In a manufacturing business with a full warehouse and a dip in sales, or on a construction site during a spell of bad weather, each employee on strike will be saving you perhaps $50 a day in wages, so the cards are not always stacked on one side. However, if you do make a stand, either on this basis or when an angry steward bursts in on you, make sure you are in the right.

Contravening the Procedure Agreement

Trade union people, particularly full-time officials, uphold procedures and rules, and this is one reason for having a local procedure agreement. If a steward or local official contravenes the agreed-upon procedures, you may be able to bring pressure to bear through the full-time or branch official. That having been said, however, be well aware that any agreement is only a piece of paper; both sides should observe it, but faced with an unexpected situation or a group of angry people, the union leaders may be unable to stick to what had been agreed upon, perhaps under quite different circumstances.

Avoiding Confrontation

Another tip is to try to take the dispute out of the realm of labor-management confrontation. Unions are aware that their demands increase costs, although they feel that in the long run cost pressure forces management to increase efficiency and investment, and hence productivity. If negotiations over rates can be translated into the estimating or quoting area and into higher prices—so that both sides can see the effect of higher prices or costs on future business—then common sense is more likely to win out.

Summary

Once things start to heat up, play it by the book. Do not panic or be stampeded into quick decisions, unless the workers are clearly right, in which case you should concede as graciously as possible. Once they are out, they are losing money. Be firm and watch them change, but keep some concessions available so that the stewards can recommend a return to work without a loss of face.

There's a tiresome young man in Bay Shore.
When his fiancée cried, "I adore
The beautiful sea!,"
He replied, "I agree,
It's pretty, but what is it for?"

MORRIS BISHOP

Summary and Work Plan

Congratulations! Either you have ploughed through the book or else you have skipped to the end to see whether it was worth your while to read all the contents. Either way you have reached the point of summary. What did the book contain? What message did it preach? What must I do now?

Each chapter has its own suggestions, and most of them have their own exercises. But what follows is a form on which you can enter your own specific action plans. Do not try to do too much—or you may be frustrated. I do not know what would be too much for you, but for me I try to do one constructive item each day. I have been doing this for years and I am so conditioned now that I get a guilty feeling if for any reason I miss out.

Your plan must be desirable, achievable, and specific. I keep emphasizing this word "specific," because less specific objectives (such as, "improve communications," "have a look at the property market," "cut down on expenses") tend to open too big an area to be satisfactorily tackled in the normal course of events. They are too general to prompt specific actions to be scheduled in with the other work. But you know all that by now, and you can either use the plan form given or make your own. The plan has five columns:

1. *Objective.* Under each chapter heading, we have entered the exercises and activities proposed, and have left space for actions that you intend to take and that are particular to your own area or function.

2. *How is it to be achieved?* What plan or method are you going to use?

3. *When is it to be started?* Who is to be involved? Will it be you alone, or will colleagues, superiors, or subordinates have a part to play?

4. *How will you know when it is achieved?* What measure, sign, or other indication will tell you when you have reached your initial targets?

5. *When was it completed?* Fill this in later, with any appropriate remarks. You will get progressively better at planning and directing these sorts of improving activities.

Following this form is a specimen diary, which you can use to extract the sections in sequence so that you have a daily, weekly, and monthly plan of improvements. Obviously you will need to write out your own form.

The rest is up to you. The book contains a good number of ideas and hints which have helped managers and supervisors to improve themselves and their activities. I can only hope that some of these ideas will prove of value to you, and I do very sincerely wish you every success.

PERSONAL ACTION PLAN (SPECIMEN)

Manager			Date	
Objective	How it is to be achieved	Start date	Controls	Finish date

SPECIMEN DIARY

PROGRAM FOR:

TASK OR ACTION	WEEK 1 M T W T F	2 M T W T F	3 M T W T F	4 M T W T F	5 M T W T F	6 M T W T F	7 M T W T F	8 M T W T F	NOTES
(LIST TASKS TO BE UNDERTAKEN)	INSERT ✓ FOR ACTION INTENDED OR REQUIRED. CROSS ✗ WHERE ACTION TAKEN. REPLAN OR REMOVE FROM LIST.								

DATE:

PREPARED BY:

Index

A

achievement, as factor aiding motivation, 84
action, as lifeblood of business, 57
active relaxation, 28
activity chart, for assessment of work, 131, 132
advertising, as step in recruiting procedure, 105
agreement by attribution, 97–98
alternatives, consideration of, in decision-making process, 59
appearance, personal
  importance of, 27–28
  as influencing behaviors, 92
appraisals of subordinates
  assessment form used for, 122–123
  communication during, need for, 116
  counseling as element of, see counseling
  conducting, 117–118
  criticism during, 116, 117
  employees' intentions prior to, 117
  importance of praise in, 117
  principles of, 123–124
areas of expertise, 86
Argenti, John, on plans, 41

assessment of work
   diary sheet for, 130–131
   work distribution chart for, 130, 135, 138
assessment form, 122
attention span, as important element in time management, 18

B

"batching"
   effects of, 54
   for improving operations, 139
   principles of, 54–55
   timing of operations and, 42
block charts, 140, 141, 142
breathing
   diaphragmatic, importance of, 29
   rhythmic, as means of relaxation, 28

C

candidate specifications, use of, in recruiting, 103, 104–105
career objectives, *see* objectives, career
career planning, manager's, 22–26
change, implementation of, through selling factors, 88–89
checklist for reviewing functions, 10
checks and controls, reduction of, for job satisfaction, 15, 85
choices, method for presenting, 90–91
classified ads, use of, in recruiting, 105
communication
   body language as type of, 93
   choices, presentation of, as important element of, 90–91
   conflict of goals as hindering, 82–83
   of decisions, use of meetings for, 66
   need for, in appraisals and counseling, 116
   with subordinates, 8–9, 14
concerns, mutual, as aids during first encounters, 92–93
conflict of goals, 82–83
consideration, as element in decision-making process, 59
consistency, behavioral, 92–93
control, manager's, over employees, 89–90
cost evaluation, 140–143
counseling
   interviews, 124
   purpose of, 124

course of action, selection of, as element in decision-making process, 60
credibility of references, 110
crises
  manager's handling of, 25
  vs. routine occurrences, 17–18
  as time wasters, 17
criticism of subordinates
  constructive, 117
  effect of, on motivation, 117
  problems caused by, 116

D

decision-making process
  choices within, presenting, 90–91
  and discipline, 57
  effects of desirability and probability on, 61, 63–64
  mechanics of, 57–61
  need of decisiveness in, 57
decisiveness, importance of, 57
definition, as element in decision-making process, 58–59
delegation of work, as manager's time-saving device, 15–16
descriptions, job, 103–104
desirability, 62–65
dialects, problems caused by, 30–31
diaphragmatic breathing, importance of, 29
diary sheets
  example of manager's, 13
  use of, for departmental time management, 130, 135, 136, 137
  use of, for personal time management, 12
discipline in recruitment, 103
discretionary time, 18
distribution charts, use of, for departmental work, 130, 135, 138
Drucker, Peter F., on factory management, 32

E

effective listening, 31
efficiency
  effect of, on organization, 147–149
  effect of, on social relationships, 151–152
  effect of, on temperament, 153, 154
  lack of, causes for, 46–47, 149

efficiency (*Continued*)
    methods for improving, 144–146
    training for, 154–155
ego needs, satisfaction of, 81
Einstein, Albert, on significance of the individual, 23
employees, new
    assignment of tasks for, 112–113
    necessary information for, 113, 114
    orientation for, 111–112
    training of, *see* training
employment, influence of, on domestic affairs, 23
evaluation, as element in decision-making process, 60
events, planning according to, 47–48
examination, as element in decision-making process, 59
expectations, past successes and failures as determinants of, 81
expertise areas, assignment of, for job satisfaction, 86
expression, importance of, 29–30

F

facts, examining, 59
failures, as determinants of expectations, 86
frequency, planning according to, 44, 46, 47

G

grievances
    avoiding, 176–178
    handling, 174–176, 178–179

H

handicapped persons, 152–153
headings, report, use of, 73–74
hierarchy, managerial, 22
human relations approach, as management style, 22

I

illustrations, use of
    in reports, 72
    in selling, 90
images, successful, portraying, 27–31
improvement of work
    block charts for, 140, 141, 142

improvement of work (*Continued*)
   cost evaluation for determining, 12
   function review as important element of, 139, 140
   skill specialization and, 140
   timing of functions as important element of, 139
   use of work distribution chart for, 139
   see also output
industrial action, 173–176
information collection, as element of decision-making process, 59
input, volume of, assessing, 44
intelligence and temperament test, as interviewing technique, 108
interviewers
   personal bias of, 103
   problems faced by, 109–110
interviews
   and candidate's career objectives, 111
   conducting, 107
   effect of, on interviewees, 105–106
   length of, 108
   references and, 110
   tests used in, 107, 110
   use of candidate specification during, 107
   use of job description during, 107

J

job descriptions, use of
   in interviews, 107
   for recruiting, 103–104
job satisfaction
   allocation of work and, 84
   expertise areas and, assignment of, 86
   new tasks and, assignment of, 85–86
   and reduction of checks and controls, 85
   responsibility and, 84–85

L

leadership, 25–26
Leavitt, H. J., on expectations, 81
linking words, use of, 73
listening, effective, 31
loading charts, planning through, 48, 50, 51
long range planning, 167–170

M

management
   assessment of, *see* assessment of work
   control as factor in, 91–92
   control figures, 85
   constraints of time in, 11
   definition of, 1, 32
   of factories, Drucker, Peter F., on, 32
   historical perspective on, 22
   improvement of, *see* improvement of work
   job satisfaction and, 22, 85
   meetings as tool for, *see* meetings
   by objectives (MBO), *see* management by objectives
   of peak loads, 52–54
   personal style and, 25
   senior, *see* senior management, dealing with
   styles of, 22
   time, *see* time management
   use of, 33
   see also planning and scheduling
management by objectives (MBO)
   definition of, 32–33
   objectives in, importance of, 33–34
managerial hierarchy, 22
managers
   achievement of objectives by, 26
   career planning for, 22–25
   definition of, 20–22
   effectiveness of, 19
   functions of, reviewing, 18
   individual, determining objectives of, 35
   lack of control over subordinates by, 89–90
   needs of, 33–34
   objectives action plan of, 36
   personal style of, 25–26
   requirement of, 87
   targets of, 35–37
   of today, 21
   trade unions and, 171–179
man-hours, management of, 159, 162–164
manpower planning
   extending, 167, 169, 170
   monthly performance control form for, 164–167, 168
   reports for, 158–162
   use of man-hours in, 162–164

manpower resources, management of, 41–55

MBO, *see* management by objectives

meetings

    attendance at, 66–67

    chairman's duties at, 67

    initial, conduct recommended for, 92–93

    necessity for, determining, 66

    preparation for, 67–69

    proposals at, introduction of, 68

    purpose of, 66–67

    use of reports during, 69–70

morale, effect of pressure on, 55

motivation

    conflicting goals as hindering, 82–83

    definition of, 77–78

    degree of employee, 78

    enhancing employee, method for, 149–151

    factors in successful, 84

    psychological factors in, 78–79

"moving averages," 44

multiple activity chart, use of, for detailed planning, 48, 49

mutual concerns, 92–93

N

needs

    company, 112

    creating, as method of selling, 87–88

    ego, 81

    personal, 33, 112, 151

new tasks, introduction of, for job satisfaction, 85–86

O

objectives

    definition and types of, 33

    effect of, on profits, 34

    management by (MBO), 32–34

    targeting, 34–37

objectives, business

    achieving, importance of time in, 23

    conflict of, 82–83

objectives, career

    conflict of, 82–83

objectives, career (*Continued*)
  consideration of, 110–111
  time element and, 23
objectives action plan, 36
organization, personal
  and delegation of work, 15–16
  need for, 7
  and time management, 12–14
orientation, importance of, 111–112
output, factors causing variation in:
  background of employees, 154
  data variations, 146
  intellectual differences of employees, 153
  layout and organization of workplace, 145, 155–156
  material variation, 146
  mental condition of employees, 154
  motivation and control, 149
  physical differences of employees, 152–153
  physical fitness of employees, 153
  redundancy of actions, 145
  skill, employee, 146–148
  social attitudes of employees, 149–151
  social relationships of employees, 151–152
Oxford English Dictionary, word statistics of, 29

P

passive relaxation, 28
peak loads, management of
  and "batching," 54
  options for, 53–54
  principles for, 52–53
performance control sheets, 164–167
personal appearance, importance of, 27–28
personal organization, *see* organization, personal
planning and scheduling
  according to events, 47–48
  according to frequency, 44, 46–47
  according to volume, 44, 45, 46
  frameworks for, 44–48
  through loading charts, 48, 50, 51
  long range, 167–170
  as part of management, 42–43
  through multiple activity chart, 48, 49
"power" words, 74

praise, as necessary element in review sessions, 117
pressure, effects of, on morale, 55
probabilities, 62–65
profits, attaining, through objectives, 34

R

ranking, as form of evaluation, 60, 62
recognition, as factor in motivation, 84
recruiting
    through advertising, 105
    candidate specification as important element of, 103, 107
    through employment service agencies, 105
    interviewing as process of, *see* interviews
    job description as important element of, 103, 107
    through staff contacts, 106
references, credibility of, 110
relaxation
    active, 28
    passive, 28
    rhythmic breathing as technique for, 28
reports
    arranging material within, 70–72
    information for, 70
    use of testimonials or illustrations in, 72
    writing, *see* writing, report
responsibility, increased, for job satisfaction, 84–85
review sessions, *see* assessment of employees
rhythmic breathing, as means of relaxation, 28

S

salary, quoting, in classified ads, 105
"sandwich technique," 117
satisfaction, job, *see* job satisfaction
scheduling
    efficiency in, 146–150
    of events, 42–43
    man-hours, 159, 162–164
    of work, 42–43
    see also planning and scheduling
self-confidence, importance of, 81, 94
self-control, importance of, 80–82

selling
    choice as factor in, 90–91
    key factors in, 88–89
    phrases to avoid in, 99
    phrases to use in, 99–100
    written proposals as aids in, 95
senior management
    characteristics of, 94
    dealing with, method for, 94–97
    definition of, 93–94
    disagreements with, handling, 94
    discretion in dealings with, 95–96
servicing, importance of, 41
shop stewards, relationships with, 172–173
situation test, as interviewing technique, 108
skill test, as interviewing technique, 107
speaking to groups
    breathing for, 29
    listening, effective, for, 31
    relaxation techniques for, 28
    voice control for, 30–31
    word selection for, 19–30
specific knowledge test, as interviewing technique, 107–108
staff performance report, 118, 119
stress interview, 107
style, personal, as factor of successful management, 25
subheadings, use of, in reports, 73–74
subordinates
    appraisal of, see appraisal of subordinates
    attitudes toward, 8–9
    buyers as, 89–90
    challenges for, 85–86
    checking work of, 15
    counseling, necessity of, 124
    criticism of, 116–117
    delegating work to, 15, 84
    grievances of, 174–179
    ideas of, 59
    interviewing, see interviews
    listening to, 31, 59, 115–116
    motivational approaches for, 78–84
    physical limitations of, 152–153
    recruiting, see recruiting
    responsibility to, 84–85

subordinates (*Continued*)
  time of, 16–18
  training of, *see* training
successes, as determinants of expectations, 81
suitability, job, as factor in motivation, 84
systems approach, as management style, 22

T

targets, *see* objectives
task list, use of, in assessment of work, 131–134
Taylor, F. W., on control, 1–3, 32
temperament and intelligence test, as interviewing technique, 108
testimonials, use of, in reports, 72
three-category concept of work, 43
three-stage concept of work, 42–43
time, constraints on
  and career planning, 23–25
  consideration of, 11–14
time, idle, 132–133
time management
  attention span as important element of, 18
  criteria for improved, 18
  delegation of work as important element in, 15–16
  and personal organization, 12–14
trade unions
  general discussion of, 171–172
  grievances and, 174–176, 178–179
  shop stewards and, 172–173
  wage bargaining with, 176
training
  demonstrating as technique for, 126–127
  efficiency of, 154–155
  method of, 125–126
  questioning trainee as technique for, 127–128

U

unions, *see* trade unions

V

voice control, importance of, 30–31
volume, planning according to, 44–46

W

weighing, as form of evaluation, 60, 61, 62
word selection
  importance of, 29–30
  misuse of, 74–75
  phrases to avoid in, 98–99
  selling phrases in, 99–100
word statistics (*Oxford English Dictionary*), 29
work
  assessment of, *see* assessment of work
  batching and, *see* "batching"
  distribution of, to subordinates, 15, 84
  efficiency of, *see* efficiency
  improvement of, *see* improvement of work
  physical limitations and, 152–153
  three-category concept of, 43
  three-stage concept of, 42–43
work distribution chart
  analysis of, 19
  example of manager's, 14
  use of, for improvement of work, 139
  use of, for time management, 12, 17
workplace, condition of, 155–156
writing, report
  focusing for, 74–75
  printing techniques for, 75
  use of headings in, 73–74
  word selection for, 73, 74